Antique Furniture Designs

By the same author

Antique Furniture Repairs
English Period Furniture

This book is dedicated to my wife

Antique Furniture Designs

Charles H. Hayward

Charles Scribner's Sons · New York

Published by Charles Scribner's Sons
New York

20 18 16 14 12 10 8 6 4 2 I/C 1 3 5 7 9 11 13 15 17 19

Printed in Great Britain.
Library of Congress Catalog Card Number 79–64524
SBN 0–684–16302–0

Contents

Foreword

In preparing these measured drawings of old furniture, in addition to giving their general details, I have endeavoured to show the way in which they were made. Apart from its usefulness to the man who makes reproductions, such knowledge is often invaluable in dating a piece, and sometimes in explaining why certain details were present and why furniture of a certain type was evolved, because practical considerations have frequently had their effect on design.

As an example of this, take the use of cocked beads around the edges of drawers, Fig. 1. They were not used because somebody thought they looked nice (though in fact they did) but because they served to protect the edges of the veneer on the drawer fronts. Or why was the framed and panelled method of construction evolved? Its attractive appearance was merely a by-product, its chief purpose being to avoid the bad effects of shrinkage when a wide expanse had to be filled. Shrinkage does no harm unless you try to stop it. By making a framework strength was ensured across the width as well as the length, and the panel, fitting dry in grooves, was free to shrink (or swell) without affecting the over-all width, Fig. 2. (Wood does not shrink in length, only across the grain.) Many other instances could be given of the influence of workshop requirements on design.

By the second half of the seventeenth century furniture-making had largely become a separate branch of woodwork, and methods of construction became more or less standardised, such methods being founded on the experience of the past. It is true that the unusual or unexpected does turn up occasionally, and it is fascinating to speculate why the maker followed his own particular ideas. Sometimes it may have been because he had to suit his method to the size of timber available to him; or it may be because he lacked the tools or appliances to follow the more usual or traditional way; or if it was a country-made item, it may have been because the maker was not familiar with the methods used in the towns. Another possibility is that the maker did not realise that the accepted methods were based on what experience had shown to be reliable, and he went his own sweet way, sometimes with unfortunate results! An example of this can sometimes be seen in early veneered work when the veneer has been taken over joints

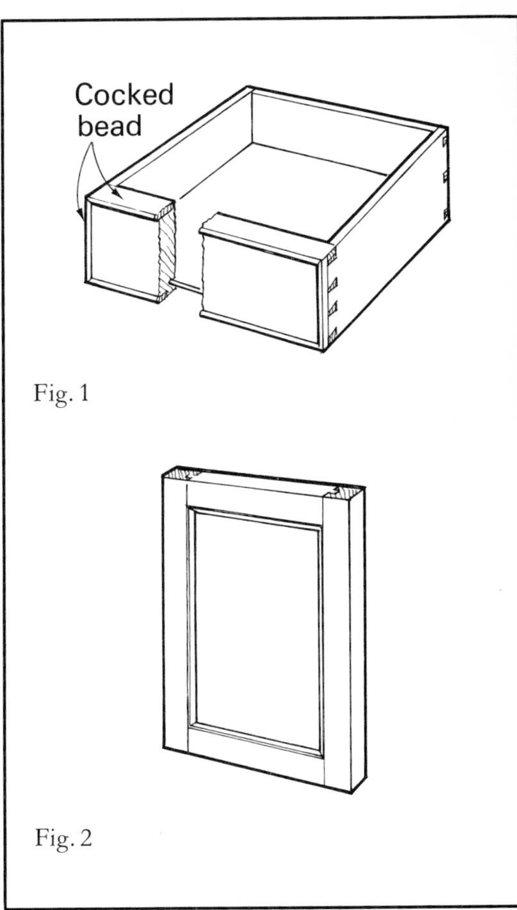

Fig. 1

Fig. 2

such as dovetails; with the loosening of the joints over the years the veneer itself has cracked or torn away, Fig. 3.

In the nature of things an item which has been in constant use for two or three hundred years or more must have suffered wear and damage. For example, I have seen drawer rails and the fronts of the drawer runners so worn that there was only a quarter of the original thickness left, Fig. 4. Mouldings may be knocked off and joints, especially in chairs, become loose. From time to time these may have been repaired (sometimes there is a repair of a repair) and in some cases the only way of making an effective repair has been to alter the construction. This can be misleading and give a false idea of how the piece was originally made.

The standardised system of construction is brought out in Shearer's *Book of Prices* published in 1788 and later. In it a chest of drawers, say, in its simplest form, is priced (the amount to be paid on a piecework basis to the cabinet-maker), and the extras to be paid for additional elaboration are given. The low price paid to the workman for making a square chest of drawers is almost unbelievable. Even allowing for the higher value of money in the second half of the eighteenth century compared with today it is obvious that a cabinet-maker must have been on close to starvation wages. It has to be remembered that, although the workman had his timber supplied to him ready cut from the log, it was anything but evenly finished. Since it was mostly cut on the pit-saw it had to be planed true before it could be smoothed and brought to a good finish. All joints had to be cut by hand and all mouldings had to be worked with moulding-planes or with the scratch-stock. Any veneering was included in the price, and the only items the cabinet-maker did not have to tackle were carving and marquetry cutting, though he had to lay the marquetry.

Of course he learnt to be artful in his methods, doing an operation by the quickest and easiest

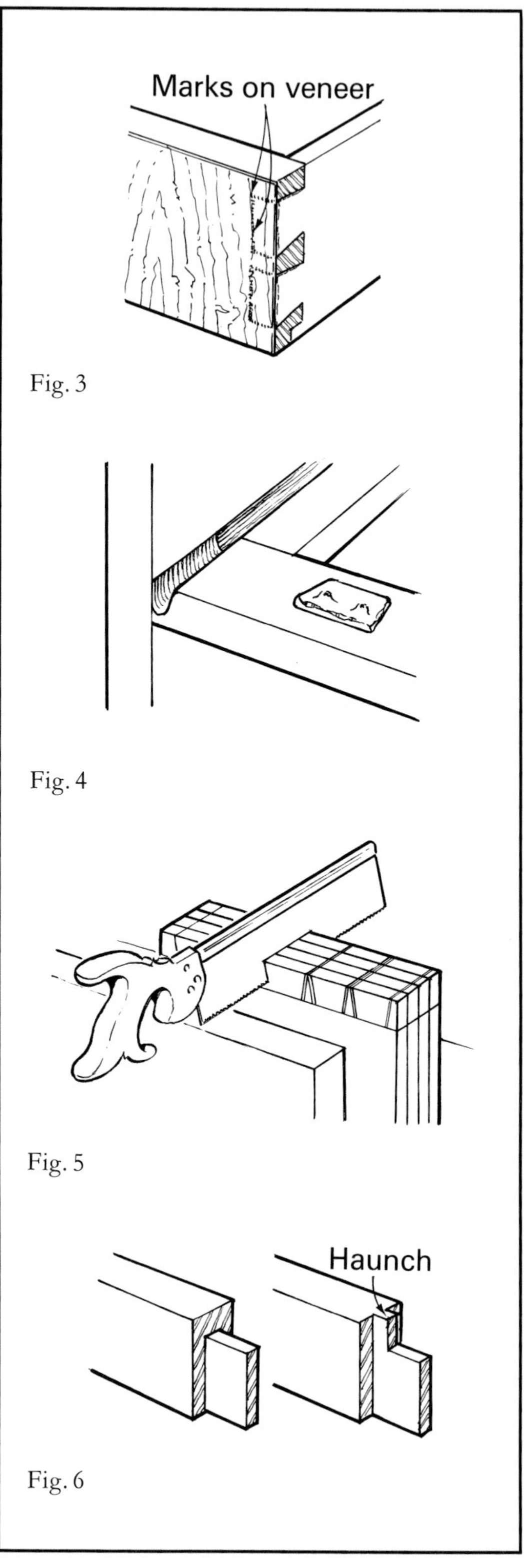

Fig. 3

Fig. 4

Fig. 5

Fig. 6

way that still guaranteed a high-quality result. Thus when a pair of chests, for example, was put in hand he would frequently cut duplicate parts at the same time. In making drawers of the same size, the sides would be cramped together and the dovetails sawn across, all in one operation, Fig. 5. Only one setting of the gauge was needed for grooving and rebating, and so all corresponding parts could be worked at the same time. The gluing operations would all be done at the same time when practicable.

In mortise and tenon joints of a framework he seldom cut a haunch to the tenon (unless it were a grooved frame and the haunch was necessary to fill in the end of the groove). Today the haunch is generally recommended as adding to the strength, but in old furniture it was the exception rather than the rule. Fig. 6.

No doubt the same system applied as I recall in a workshop early in the present century. When a big job had to be assembled the man at the next bench gave a hand in heating joints, fixing cramps, testing, etc., and if he had no immediate recompense he had corresponding help when he had a similar job to assemble himself.

Anyone interested in making reproductions will, if a purist, want to follow the methods used at the appropriate period, but he will frequently find himself in difficulties because many timbers are no longer available – at any rate in solid form. Frequently he will have to use timber salvaged from second-hand furniture which has ended its useful life. Old joints may have to be cut out and screw- or nail-holes made good, but such wood is usually in good condition and is excellent for the purpose.

Another consideration is that of the tools that were in use at the period the reproduction represents – or perhaps a more useful way of looking at it is that of the tools that were *not* available at the time. In some operations it makes little difference. For instance, a groove could be cut with a modern metal plough plane and the result could not be detected as different from that worked with an old wood grooving plane. The groove could even be cut on a machine spindle-moulder or high-speed router providing the groove were taken right through the entire length (you could not stop a groove if a plough plane were used). There is, however, a certain uniformity about a moulding worked by machine as compared with hand methods, and in some cases marks across the grain can be detected, the result of the rotary action of the cutter, expecially if the wood has been taken too rapidly across the cutter. If such marks do appear on the surface they should be taken out by dampening the surface with hot water, leaving to dry, then glasspapering, using a wood rubber of the reverse shape to that of the moulding. In any case, early oak period reproduction mouldings should never be machined. The result is too regular.

Flat surfaces which have been machine-planed should always be planed by hand afterwards and scraped. If, as sometimes happens, the cutters of the planer have been gashed, great ridges will be left on the surface and it is necessary to dampen as described above, and then plane by hand.

In my time I have had to make a good many reproductions of period pieces, and in the early days when there was an almost unlimited supply of prime timbers we were able to follow traditional methods of construction, but in later years it has become more difficult and I am afraid that for some parts plywood or blockboard have had to be used, the surface being veneered and the edges lipped with solid wood. This sometimes meant that the traditional construction has had to be adapted to suit the material. But when joints were necessarily exposed, in drawer dovetails and certain framing parts, we always used solid timber and traditional construction.

In some respects modern materials have their advantages; they are free from shrinkage and there is less liability for cracks and splits to develop. But such timbers as prime mahogany have little movement and, in any case, the old cabinet-makers kept it in stock to season out thoroughly before using it. If they hadn't done this, the task of the repairer today would be still more difficult, as the movement of the wood would have been greater.

The modern furniture-making workshop is very different from the corresponding workshop of sixty or seventy years ago. Practically every operation, jointing, working mouldings or similar details, veneering, cleaning up, is machined; even assembling is done with special appliances. At the same time, there are still some master craftsmen turning out first-class individual period pieces which are termed reproductions. Additionally there are many men who specialise in restoration work. The present high prices fetched by old furniture have indeed resulted in a trade in which the jobs of the repairer, the reproduction maker and the converter have become curiously mixed, and it is sometimes difficult to decide whether an item has been given a new lease of life by the antique tradesman or is purely the product of the faker. In fact there have been times when I have never been quite sure whether some of the work I have been involved in came under the heading of what may euphemistically be described as reproduction, or whether to give myself virtuous airs and claim the merit of having saved decrepit old furniture from further deterioration or destruction. However, I hope that the details given in the drawings in this book, and the notes on construction, will be of some help to the reader in assessing the authenticity of a piece, or help a craftsman to make an item by traditional methods. Interested readers will find this subject developed more fully in another of my books, *Antique or Fake?*

Charles H. Hayward
Letchworth, 1979

Oak table, about 1690

Fig. 1 Oak table

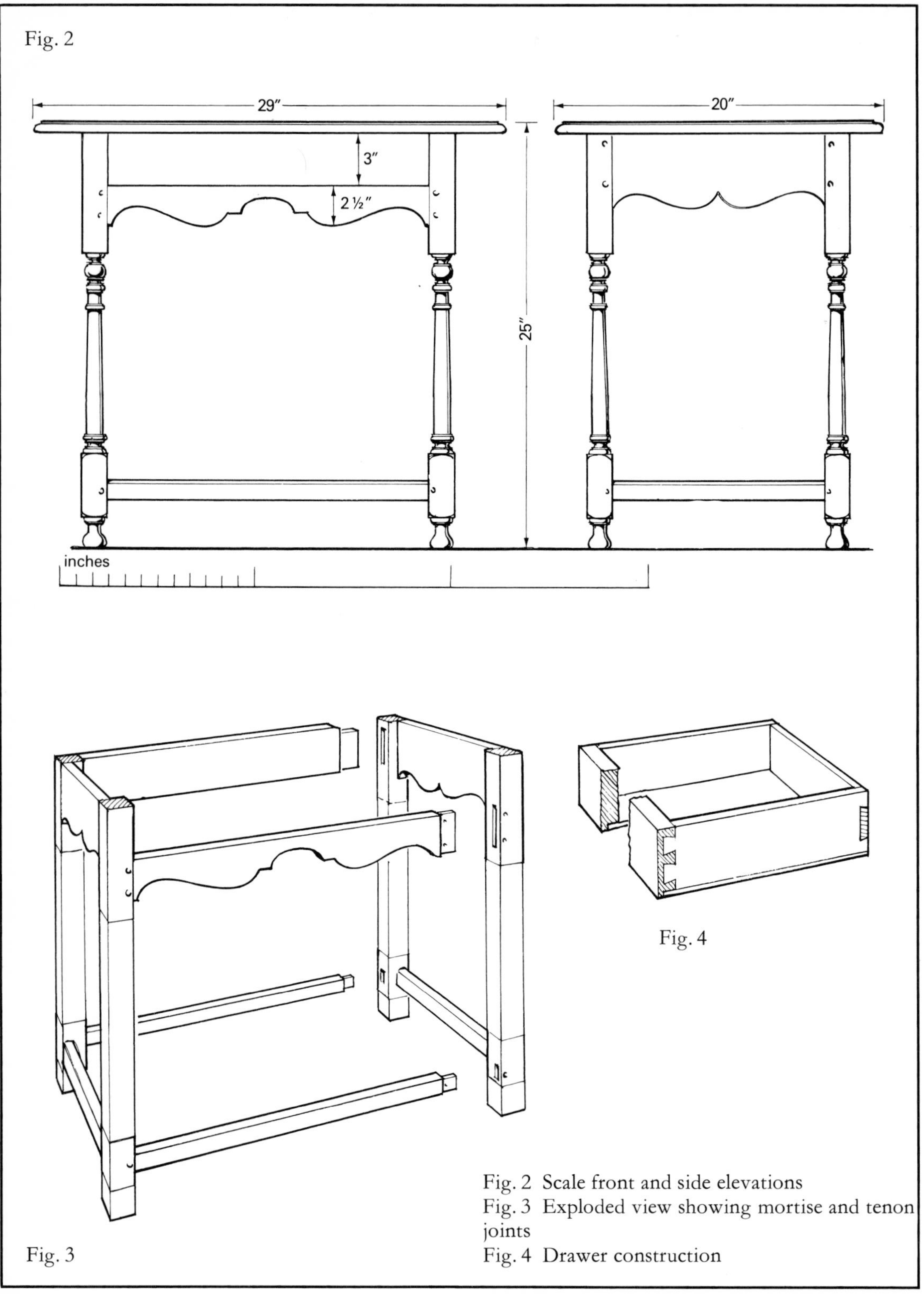

Fig. 2 Scale front and side elevations
Fig. 3 Exploded view showing mortise and tenon joints
Fig. 4 Drawer construction

Drawn from the original in the possession of Collins Antiques Limited, Wheathampstead.

It was not until the second half of the seventeenth century that small tables became common. Hitherto the large table in the hall which might accommodate a dozen to two dozen diners had been mostly used, but during the seventeenth century the idea of dining in private gradually grew, and so came the gate-leg table and many varieties of the side or occasional table. Early models were invariably in oak, but after the Restoration walnut was used, with the flat surfaces veneered, often with marquetry decoration. At the same time oak was still used for the simpler and less expensive tables. Oak was plentiful in the country and was cheaper than walnut, and, since it was used in the solid, called for nothing more than traditional construction.

Fig. 1 shows a table probably made towards the end of the century, with turned baluster legs mortised to receive rails and stretchers. A feature worth noting is that there is no top front rail such as was used later. Even many walnut writing-tables made in the early years of the eighteenth century had the same omission, and it was not until about 1720 that a top rail was usually fitted. In this sense it may be said that the top itself formed part of the main construction instead of being added afterwards as a separate item.

Fig. 4 shows the drawer construction with rather coarse dovetails lapped at the front and through at the back. The grain of the bottom runs from front to back, and it fits beneath the sides and back, and in a rebate in the front. Runners are glued and nailed to the side rails with guides to control side movement.

Oak chair-table, late mid-17th century

Drawn from the original at the Victoria and Albert Museum, South Kensington.

This is an early example of a dual-purpose piece of furniture, the table-top being pivoted so that it can be turned back to form a back to the chair. Six boards, ⅝in. thick, form the top, cross-battens with shaped edges being used to hold them together. Turned dowels, which pass through both the battens and the arms, enable the top to pivot, and there are corresponding holes in the front of the arms and battens to enable the top to be locked, when flat. As can be seen from Fig. 1, the top is not quite circular. Oak is used throughout, and the

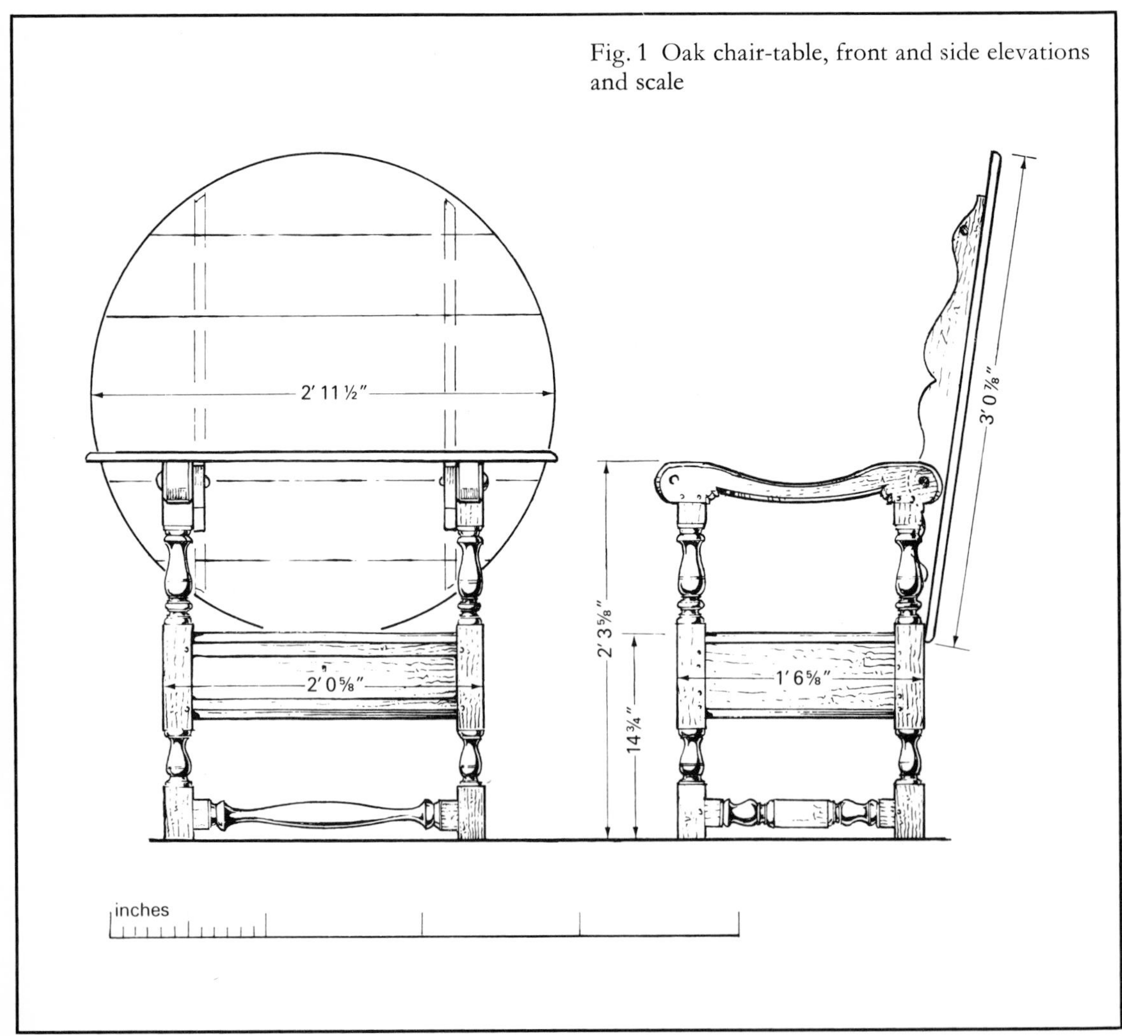

Fig. 1 Oak chair-table, front and side elevations and scale

design and workmanship suggest a capable craftsman. Mortise and tenon joints are used for the main framework, all held together by pegs. Runners for the drawer are fitted to the side rails, and there are guides to prevent side movement as the drawer is opened.

Details of the drawer are given in Fig. 3, and it will be seen that lapped-dovetails are used at the front, and through-dovetails at the rear. As the bottom is fixed immediately beneath the sides and back, and in a rebate in the front, there is no clearance beneath and it necessarily scrapes on the lower front drawer rail as it is opened.

Fig. 2 Cut-away sketch showing main parts
Fig. 3 Details of the drawer construction
Fig. 4 Arm and turning details

Presumably the shaping of the arms was not entirely for appearance, though this does enhance them, but largely to give positive support to the top at front and rear. It will be realised that if the top were to cast, it might bed down on the middle of straight arms, and be liable to rock. All mortise and tenon joints are pegged.

The photograph used as the frontispiece to this book shows another example of a chair-table, also from the Victoria and Albert Museum.

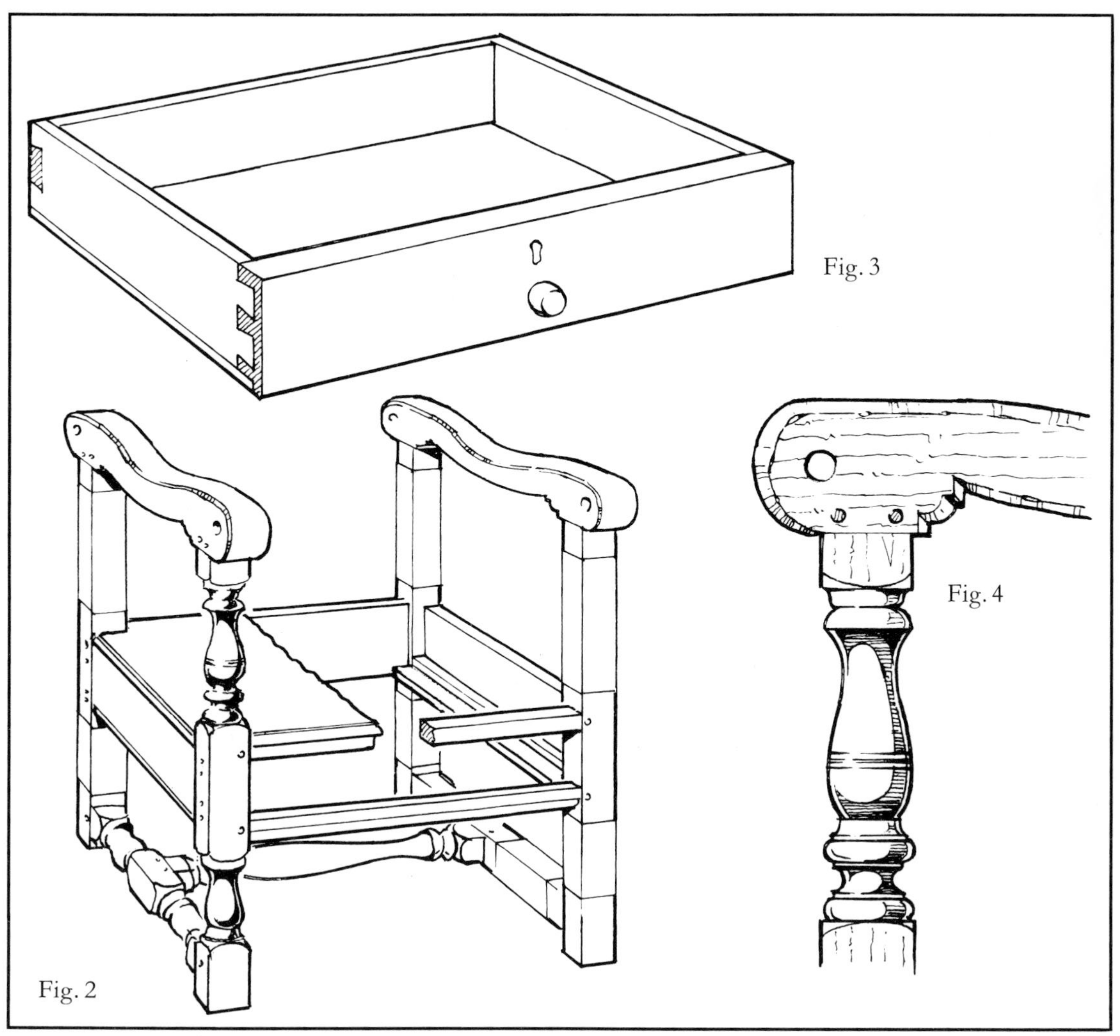

Walnut chest of drawers, about 1700

Fig. 1 Walnut chest of drawers

Drawn from the original in the possession of Collins Antiques Limited, Wheathampstead.

Except for one or two details this chest follows the normal construction in general use in the early eighteenth century. Top and bottom are lap-dovetailed to the ends, and the top itself forms part of the structure (later the tendency was for rails to be dovetailed to the ends and a separate top added above). To enable a fairly wide moulding to be fitted around the top, a thicknessing piece has been added beneath the top at the front (A, Fig.3). A similar idea was followed at the front of the ends, these being thicknessed as at B, Fig. 3, and a flat rounded moulding added as shown. Drawer rails are tenoned to the ends.

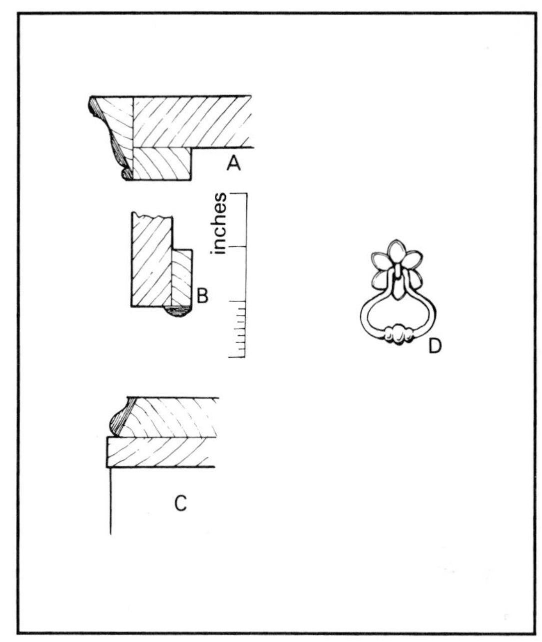

Fig. 3 (above) Enlarged details. **A** section through top moulding; **B** plain section through end; **C** base moulding; **D** handle

One of the unusual features of this piece is the arrangement of the drawers. The bottoms are fixed to the lower edges of the sides and back, and, to prevent the bottoms scraping as they are withdrawn, the runners are set about $\frac{1}{4}$in. above the level of the drawer rails, the fronts

Fig. 2 (below) Front and side elevations

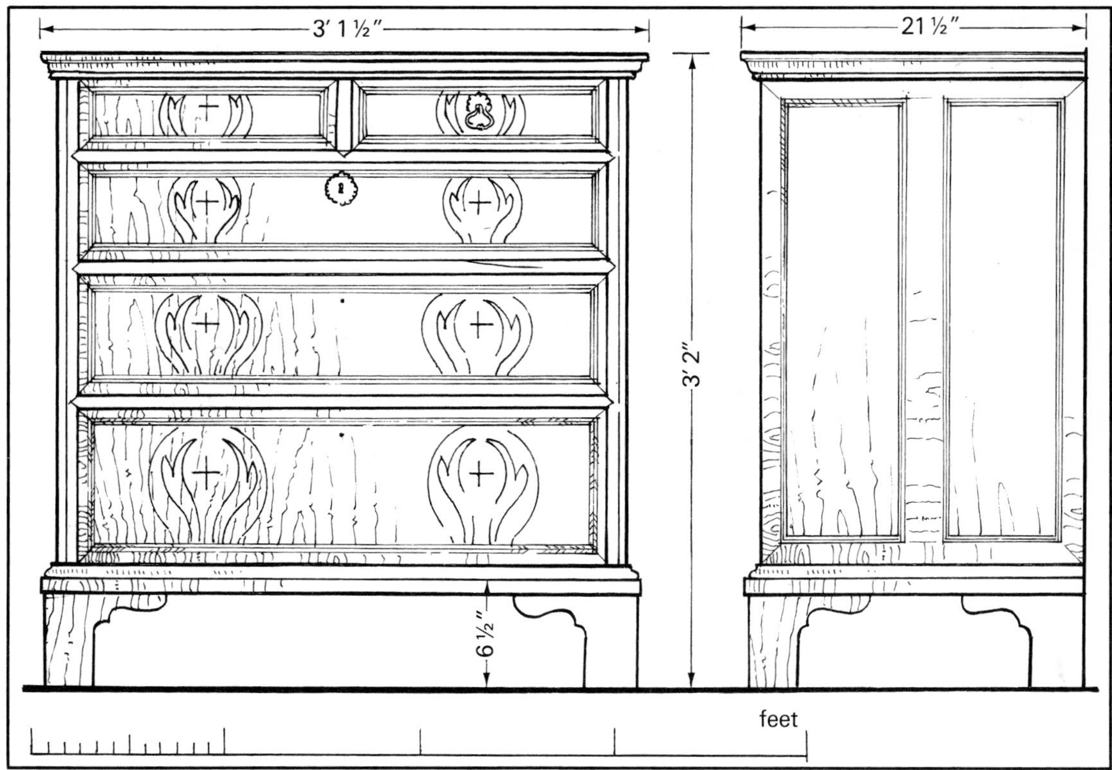

projecting downwards by a corresponding amount. Thus the bottoms clear the drawer rails though they actually bear on the runners at the sides.

All carcase parts are in softwood, plain butt joints being used to make up the width. Thicknessing pieces are added, as already outlined, and the cross-grained top moulding added. Probably the moulding was made up separately, the cross-grained walnut being glued to a softwood groundwork. After being worked it would be mitred round. Top veneer would be laid over the whole. The veneer on the ends would be more conveniently done beforehand.

It is an interesting speculation as to the method used by the craftsman to veneer the top, which is treated in a decorative way with an elliptical centre and herring-bone inlays and cross-banding. One way would have been to assemble the veneers on a flat board on which the design had been drawn, and then lay the whole in a single operation, with a caul. More likely, however, he drew the design on the actual top and laid the veneers piecemeal, starting with the central elliptical panel. This may have been cut to shape beforehand, then pressed down, or it may have been cut out full to size, laid, then

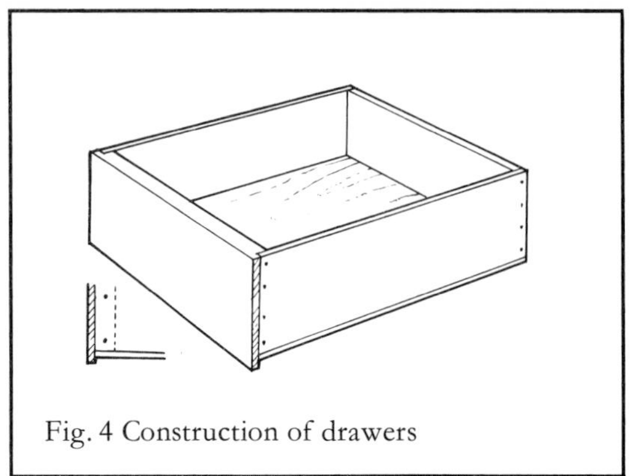

Fig. 4 Construction of drawers

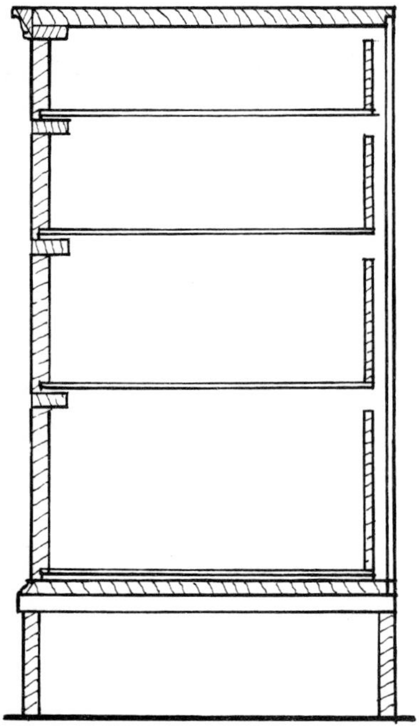

Fig. 5 Side section of the chest

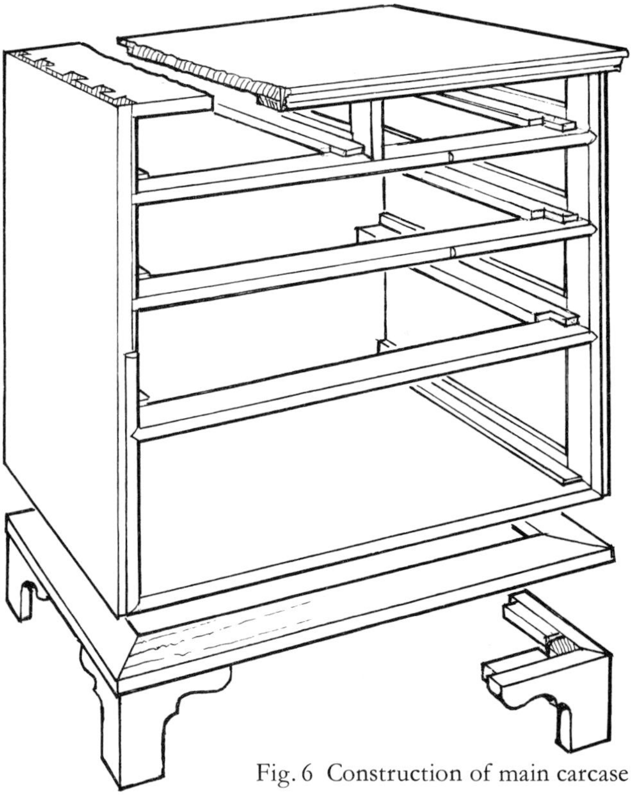

Fig. 6 Construction of main carcase

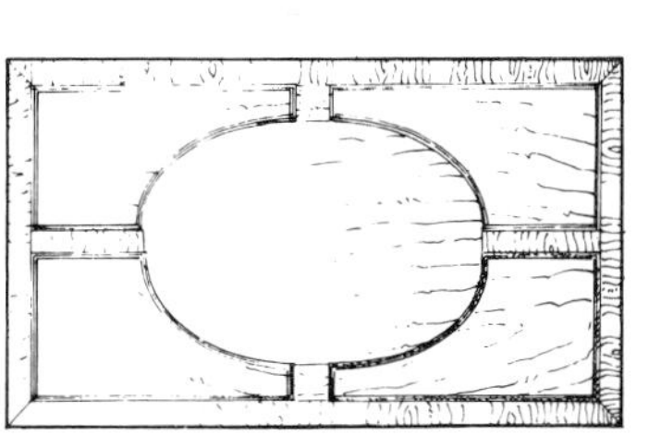

Fig. 7 Plan of top showing decorative arrangement

trimmed round with a chisel or knife, a template of the shape being used. This would be done immediately so that the waste could be peeled away, before the glue had set hard. The herring-bone banding would be fitted up to this elliptical panel. As the bandings were invariably made in straight lengths, it would have been necessary to separate the banding along the centre, because there is a boxwood line along each side which would resist bending, especially as the banding is in the region of $\frac{3}{8}$in. wide. This is the method makers of reproduction furniture and repairers have to follow (except when the curve is very acute, in which case the banding has to be specially made in curved form). Fine pins knocked partially into the groundwork at the outside would hold the banding in position whilst the glue was setting. Then the four corner panels would be fitted up to the herring-bone bandings. At the front, back, and two sides are broad cross-bandings, and the herring-bone inlays continue at each side. Finally the main cross-banding around the edges would be laid, also the herring-bone inlays, all the corners being mitred.

A second unusual feature of the chest is the grain direction of the bracket feet. This was usually horizontal, because the feet were frequently in solid walnut. Here the feet are veneered but the grain is vertical, the groundwork beneath being of softwood with horizontal grain. It is quite possible that they are replacements, especially as they are attached to a mitred frame which in itself is an unusual arrangement, the feet being normally fixed directly to the bottom of the carcase.

It will be seen that the carcase ends also have a decorative arrangement of veneers (Fig. 2) with cross-bandings and herring-bone inlays, and it is curious to notice that the boxwood lines at each side of the herring-bone must have been laid separately. This is shown by the fact that, although the herring-bone is mitred at the corners, the boxwood lines are butted together. It seems an odd method, as surely it would have been much easier to have made up the entire banding, including the boxwood lines, and mitre the whole at the corners?

Whilst on the subject of veneering and inlaying, it is worth pausing to consider how the craftsman dealt with the curved inlay boxwood lines in the drawer fronts. At first glance it might appear that the work was done by the marquetry cutter, and the inlaid veneers then laid as a whole. Close examination shows however that this could not have been the method used, because at the acute points where two curves meet, one piece of boxwood is merely butted against the other (and not very neatly at that). Had it been cut on the marquetry donkey, the entire boxwood would have been in one piece without joints. Then, having laid the veneers, the craftsman cut in the recesses for the inlay lines, using either a narrow chisel or some similar tool, worked against a template of thin wood with a scratching or scraping action. Each drawer front would have needed three templates, which would have been reversed to enable each group of inlays to be completed. The actual inlay lines would have been prepared as a straight line and bent to fit into the recess when being glued. Finally the craftsman would have run his cutting gauge around all four sides, cutting through the veneer, thus enabling the herring-bone and cross-banding to be added.

Architectural-type mirror, early 18th century

Fig. 1

Drawn from the original in the possession of Phillips of Hitchin (Antiques) Limited

There were three main types of mirror frame made during the Queen Anne period; that with cross-grained moulded frame, generally with double-quadrant top corners, and with a fretted heading of which that on page 32 is an example; the cushion type with a wide framework generally of rounded section (hence the term); and the architectural type of which Fig. 1 is a good example. The combination of polished natural walnut with carved and gilt mouldings is specially rich and satisfying. The mirror is described by the term 'architectural' because the classical pediment with its carved mouldings and shaped members imitates details found in many buildings of the period. This mirror is water gilt; the technique involves the use of gesso and subsequent burnishing. Readers making a reproduction of the mirror may prefer the simpler alternative of oil gilding, though the result would not be so brilliant or satisfying as water gilding.

There is nothing specially involved in the main construction. As shown in Fig. 2 there is a simple square-edged frame put together with mortise and tenon joints, with an applied moulding to form the rebate for the glass, and with applied pieces at the outside to enable the projecting breaks and shaping to be worked. This is shown clearly in Fig. 2. Sometimes the framework included the whole of the lower shaping but often an applied piece was planted on as shown. At the top the framework was taken up as far as the main horizontal cornice moulding, the pediment above being a separate piece fixed in a rebate at the top of the framework and held with screws.

When this frame was made, Scotch glue was the usual adhesive for veneering, and in all probability the hammer method was used. In this method any jointing was done by allowing the veneers to overlap and cutting through both thicknesses with a thin chisel, removing the waste, and pressing down afresh. The upper waste strip had only to be peeled away, but to remove the other it was necessary to raise the veneer to reveal the waste strip beneath. As subsequent drying out tended to cause shrinkage, a strip of paper would have been glued over the joint. Today we would use gummed tape which is much more convenient and is removed more easily later.

For those not familiar with the term 'hammer veneering', the veneering hammer consists of a brass strip about 5in. long held in a wooden stock with handle as shown in Fig. 3. Both groundwork and veneer having been given a coat of glue, the veneer was placed in position, roughly smoothed down with the hands, and about one half of it lightly dampened. A warm flat iron was passed over the surface to heat the glue beneath, and the veneering hammer was then worked over the surface with a zigzag movement, squeezing out surplus glue beneath and forcing the veneer closely down on to the groundwork.

Fig. 2 Front and side elevations with scale

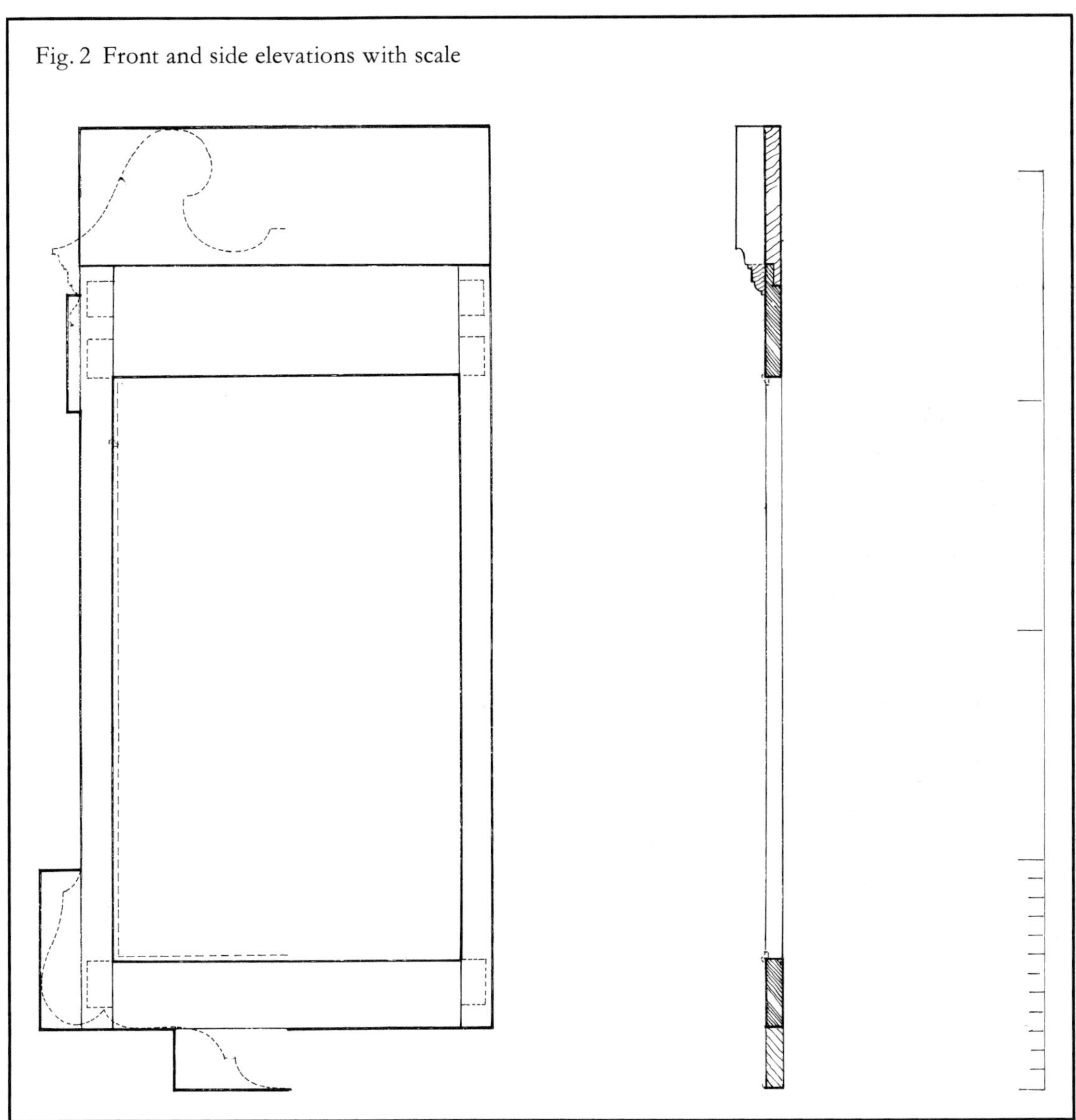

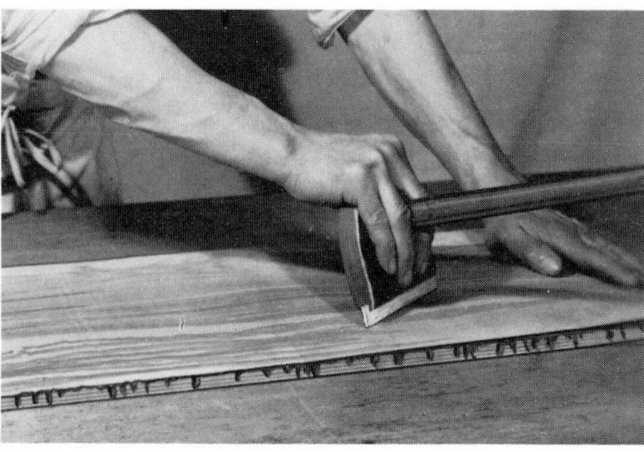

Fig. 3 Pressing down veneer with the veneering hammer

The veneer being laid, the various mouldings, straight and curved, would be prepared. Straight members were usually worked with moulding planes, but curved portions would need the scratch-stock, though the large shaped cornice would probably have been cut mainly with carving tools. The scratch-stock could have been used for the main part, but carving tools would certainly have been needed at the acute curves at the top. All carved parts, with the exception of the mouldings themselves, would have been cut in separate blocks and planted on afterwards.

In the case of the carved mouldings, the usual carver's practice was no doubt followed, in that the carver selected a minimum of tools and made downward stabs to outline the leaf and other shapes. He then eased away the adjoining parts with sloping cuts, using as few cuts as possible. This not only made for economy of movement, but also gave the work a spontaneous and spirited character. The following application of gesso inevitably had the effect of filling up the pattern – in fact in some work it is now almost impossible to discern what the original pattern was like.

As this application of gesso in the gilding process was somewhat messy, it would have been necessary to protect the surface of the veneered portions, and at that period no doubt pieces of paper were stuck over the veneer with glue size. Today pieces of transparent adhesive tape would be a simpler alternative.

Card table with concertina extension, about 1715

Fig. 1 Card table with back flap raised to show surface

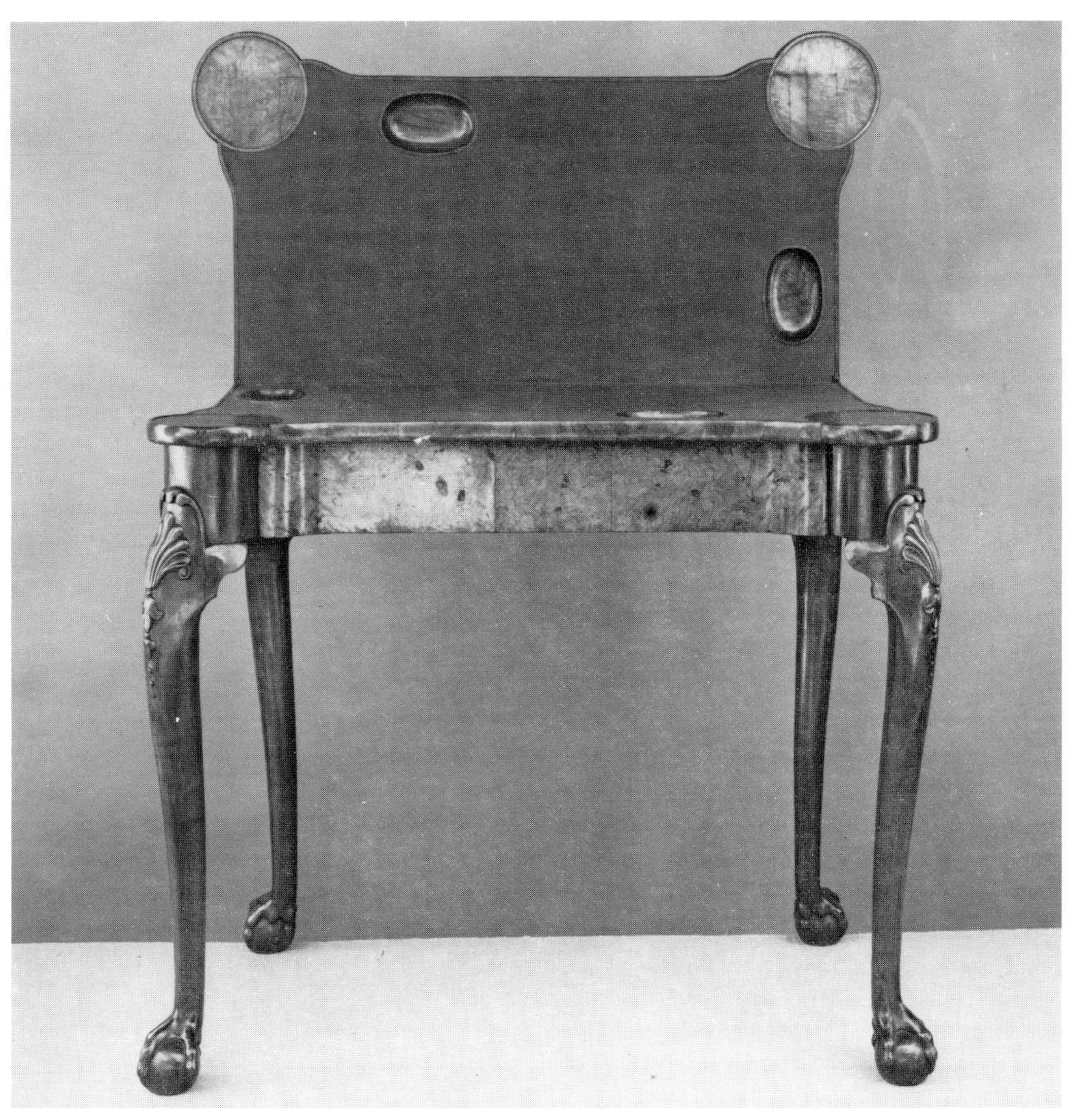

Drawn from the original at the Victoria and Albert Museum, South Kensington.

An obvious feature of a table of this kind is that, when opened, the top doubles its area, forming an approximate square. Various methods of supporting the hinged top have been used, in some cases one back leg, and in others both, being pivoted on knuckle joints cut in wood. The type most highly prized, however, had what is known as concertina action, both legs moving backwards as a whole, being attached to hinged rails at each side. At two of the joints, backflap hinges were used, but at the middle, where they would look unsightly, a special form of centre hinge with offset centres was used. It is true that, in a few rare cases, knuckle joints cut in wood were used throughout, but although two at each side were of normal pattern, the centre ones had to be specially designed to fold into an acute angle. Unless this were done, the moving parts could not be sufficiently long to give the required extension. Some years ago I had one of these tables in for repair, but the piece was in such a bad way, the result partly of wear, but mainly due to the ravages of the furniture beetle, that all the moving parts had to be completely renewed.

In the table in Fig. 1, metal hinges were used, the folding action being shown in Fig. 3. It will be noted that the front rail is fixed rigidly to the legs and to the side rails. The two back legs with their joining rail, however, are independent and are joined to the front framework by the hinged rails. Thus, in the closed position, the side rails attached to the front legs merely touch the back legs, without any joints. When opened, the hinged rails form straight side rails and are held rigid by a slide which works in grooves and is pulled backwards (Fig. 3). To prevent it from being moved too far the grooves are stopped. Knowing that a stopped groove was awkward to work, however, the craftsman worked the grooves right through, enabling him to use the plough, and glued in stops as shown.

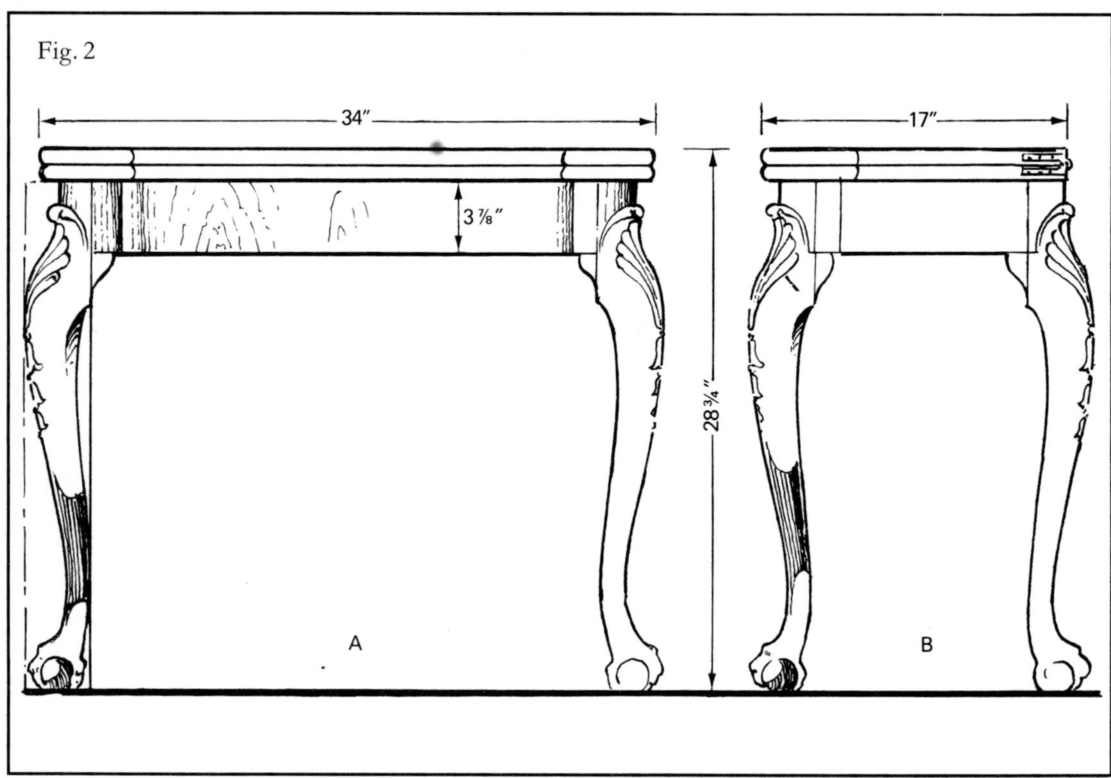

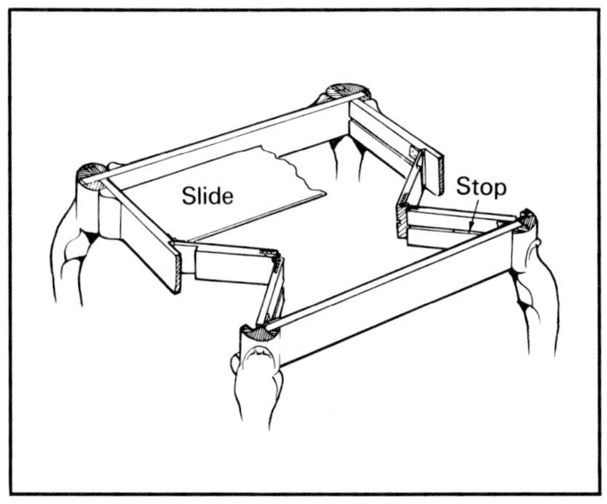

Fig. 3 (above) Top removed showing concertina movement

Fig. 2 (below, left and right) **A** front elevation; **B** side elevation; **C** plan of front corner, top removed; **D** plan of rear corner, top removed; **E** table in folded position; **F** corner of hinged top; **G** inner top surface

A point to note is that where the centre-hinged rails join the front rails, a form of halving is cut to enable the moving rails to fold together when in the closed position. To make sure of this, the length of the halving is slightly greater than the combined thickness of the two moving rails.

In common with all cabriole legs, the shape has to be cut from a square of timber (shown to the left in the elevation in Fig. 2 and in the plan view). It would be impossible to tenon the rails into the front legs because, owing to the plan shape, they would have to be set too far in. In all probability then the arrangement in Fig. 4 was followed. I say 'in all probability' because, unless the table is dismantled, it is impossible to see the actual construction. Examination of the underside shows that the rails meet each other and this means that the top square of the leg stands outside the corner of the framing rails. Consequently, to form a strong joint for the legs, one rail is through-tenoned to the other as shown in Fig. 4, and the leg square glued and

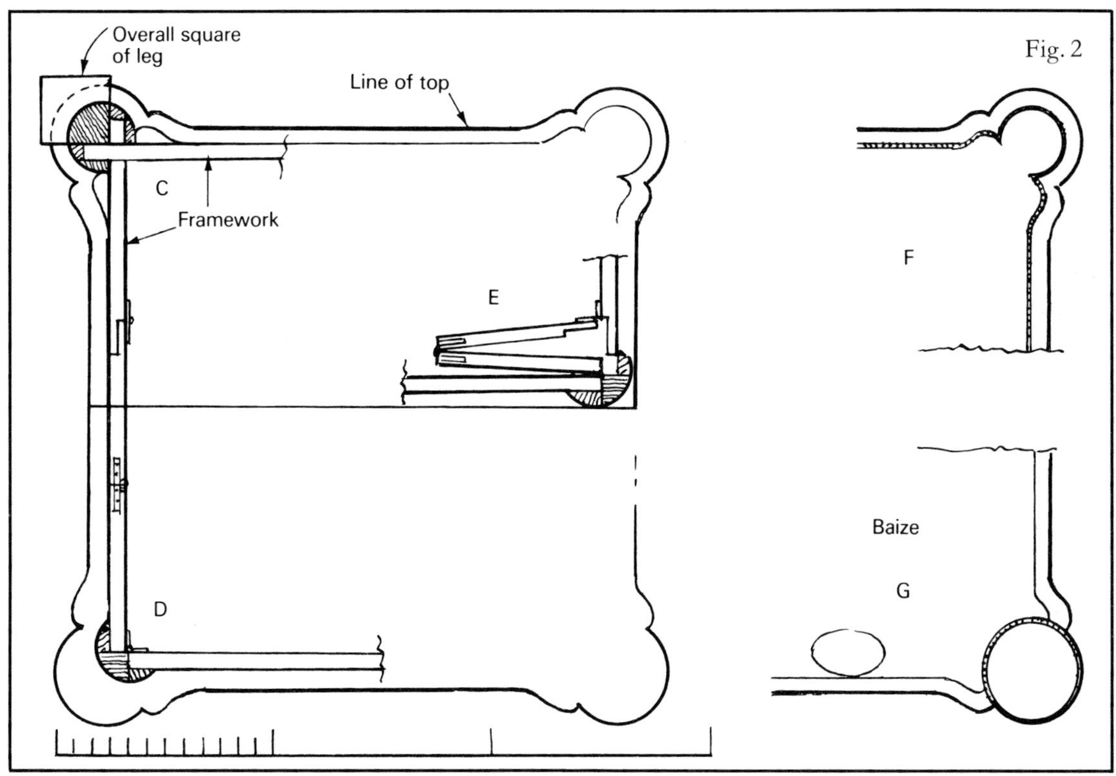

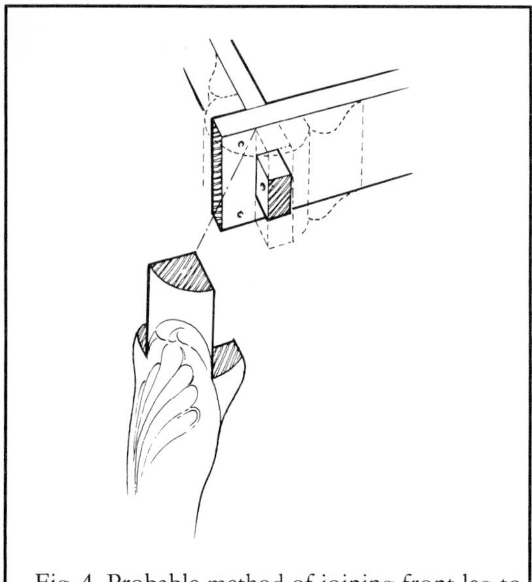

Fig. 4 Probable method of joining front leg to framework

screwed to the outer angle so formed. Alternatively the two rails could have been halved together, but this would not be so strong. Since the circular shape and the ogee have to be continued round the sides, blocks would have been glued on, as shown by the dotted lines in Fig. 4. These would have to be veneered, and no doubt the craftsman kept the projections of the rails about $\frac{1}{8}$in. short so that thin slips could be glued on, thus avoiding veneering over the end grain of the rail projections.

A rather different arrangement had to be made at the back legs. They had to be set farther in because otherwise, in the closed position, the top squares of the legs would project beyond the side rails owing to the shaping. In fact the back rail is tenoned into the squares of the legs. There is of course no jointing at the sides, the rails being hinged.

Both tops are edged with walnut to enable the flat rounded moulding to be worked, and the hinged one is veneered on the upper surface with walnut, with a herring-bone banding and outer cross-banding set around the edge. To enable the shape to be negotiated, the two parts of the herring-bone would have been separated, enabling them to bend. On the inside, the entire surface is covered over with baize and there is a cross-banding of veneer at the edges. Hollow depressions for money or counters are set in at each rounded corner, and an elliptical depression to the right along each side. Walnut blocks about $\frac{1}{2}$in. thick would be recessed in, the hollow shape cut, and the baize taken up to the edges.

Today baize would be put down with wallpaper paste made up to double strength to give a strong bond, and to avoid too wet a mix which might penetrate the baize. Only the wood would be pasted, not the baize. The latter would be thumb-nailed up to the banding, raised to enable the shape to be cut, and then pressed down finally. Probably a form of thick flour paste was used originally.

Anyone making a reproduction of the table could omit much of the carving on the knees of the legs if necessary. In fact the shaping could end level with the lower edges of the rails in line with the applied ear pieces.

Mahogany gate-leg table, 18th century

Fig. 1 Mahogany gate-leg table

Drawn from the original at the Victoria and Albert Museum

As an example of delicacy and lightness of construction this table is quite remarkable. That it should have survived in such good condition is equally so. Legs and stretcher rails are all turned from squares measuring no more than $\frac{7}{8}$in. and one can only assume that it has always lived a sheltered life in a polite drawing-room, and has never had to face the rough and tumble that so often goes with bringing up a young family, or the boisterous habits of some of its less relaxed and temperate members.

The turnery is of a high quality, and must have been the work of a skilled craftsman. The finished length of the legs is in the region of 2ft. 3in. and with slender squares of $\frac{7}{8}$in. only, the whip at the centre would have been considerable. No doubt the turner used a steady to resist this, but even so a part near the centre middle had to be turned before the steady could be used. In any case the liability of the wood to bounce even with the steady in use would have been quite marked.

It was, no doubt, the development of chair-making as a separate trade from cabinet-making that raised turnery to a high standard, and the turner was a specialist in his own trade, as distinct from the general chair-maker who made other parts, straight and shaped, and assembled them. The maker of this table would have had his turning done by such a specialist. It was by the middle of the eighteenth century that the treadle lathe with flywheel had superseded the pole lathe (see *Dictionary of Tools* by R. A. Salaman) and the probability was that the turning was done on such a lathe.

All the joints are of the stub-tenon type as

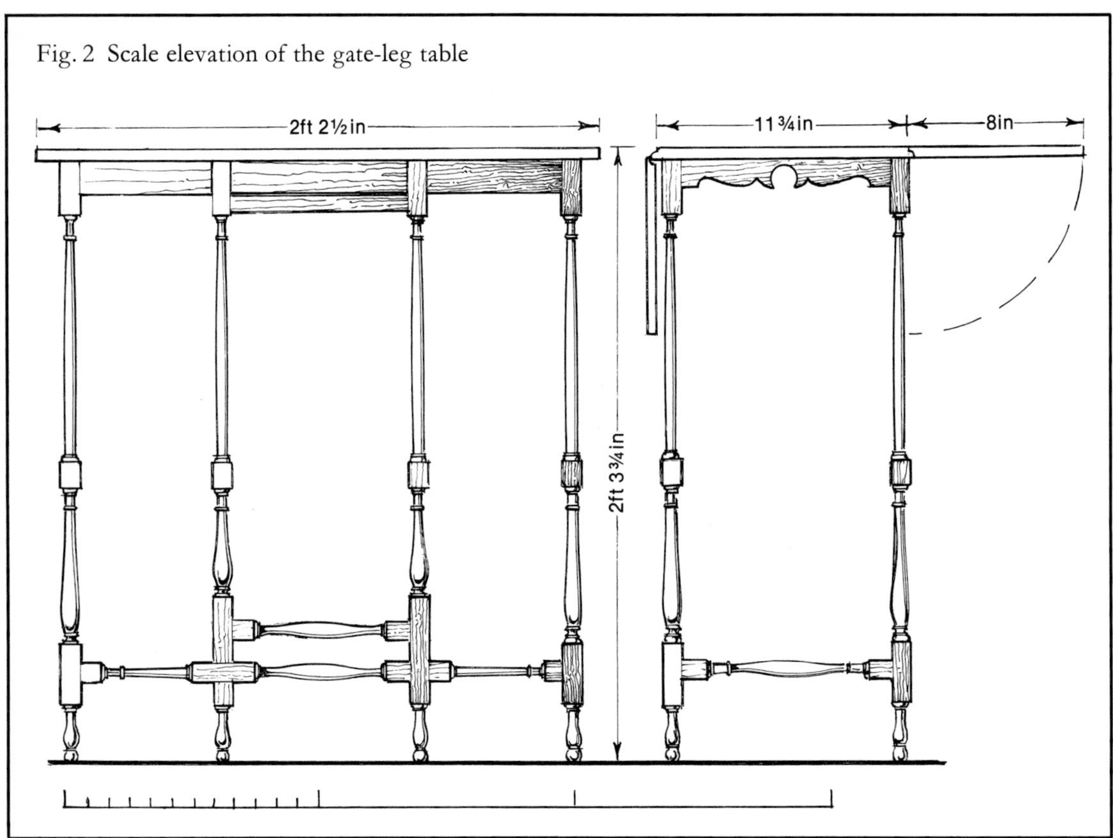

Fig. 2 Scale elevation of the gate-leg table

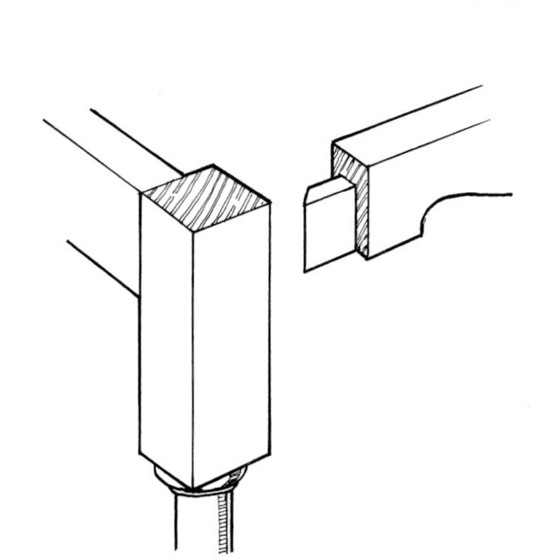

Fig. 3 Stub-tenon joints used throughout the table framework

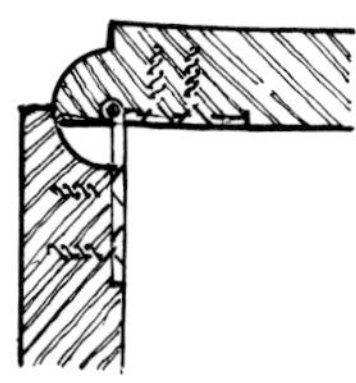

Fig. 4 Rule joint used between main top and flaps

shown in Fig. 3, and in all probability the pivoting members of the gates had dowels turned at top and bottom, in which case they must have been placed in position when the main framework was assembled. Or the craftsman may have been artful, and bored a hole at the top of the leg and a corresponding hole right through the top rail and passed a dowel in afterwards. He could, in fact, have followed a similar idea at the bottom, since the foot is a separate item which could have had a long dowel turned at the top, this being passed right through a hole in the stretcher rail and into a corresponding hole at the bottom of the leg. In this case only that part of the dowel passing through the stretcher would have been glued.

Tops are ½in. thick and the flaps are pivoted to the main top with the rule joint as shown in Fig. 4.

As a passing note, one wonders why the designer left intermediate squares on the legs. Normally such squares are left to enable a rail to be tenoned in, but obviously this is not true in the present case. Presumably he thought it looked more attractive to turn two separate parts to the leg and separate them by leaving squares.

Walnut mirror, about 1714

Fig. 1 Walnut mirror

Drawn from the original in the possession of Phillips of Hitchin (Antiques) Limited.

This is fairly typical of one type of mirror-frame being made in the early years of the eighteenth century. The main frame has a facing of cross-grained walnut worked to an ogee section, mounted on a softwood frame-work and veneered at the outer edge. Double-quadrant top corners to the moulded frame-work were common practice. The cresting, too, is of the kind often found at the period, though in many cases the shaped edges also projected at the sides; the cresting was sometimes repeated with variations at the bottom. Most mirrors were small because the cost of the mirror itself was high – frequently more than that of the frame to which it was fitted. It was no doubt due to this, and to the difficulty of producing a large mirror, that the frame was frequently jointed as in the present example, though often the upper portion was ornamented in some way.

The construction calls for some comment because it is not so obvious as it might, at first, appear. The bottom corners present no difficulty; a simple mortise and tenon joint is used, (see D, Fig. 2) and the walnut facing mitred and glued over it. E, Fig. 2 shows the section through the sides and bottom, but at the top a wider rail is used, the reason being that the double-quadrant corners would make it impossible (or difficult) to work out suitable jointing. By the arrangement shown at D, the top corners can have strong mortise and tenon joints, and, since the inner edges of both rail and stiles are level with the glass rebate formed by the applied moulding, the glass can continue right into the square corners without having to be cut to the double-quadrant shape, always an awkward job. No doubt the glazier expressed himself feelingly on the subject. Made in this way, the glass could be slipped in from the back in the usual way, the rebate being blacked beforehand so that it did not show a white reflection. The dovetailed mid-rail would have to be added afterwards when the back itself was added.

At the top the cresting could either stand above the top rail or it could be fitted into a rebate. In any case it is stiffened by an upright let into the top rail.

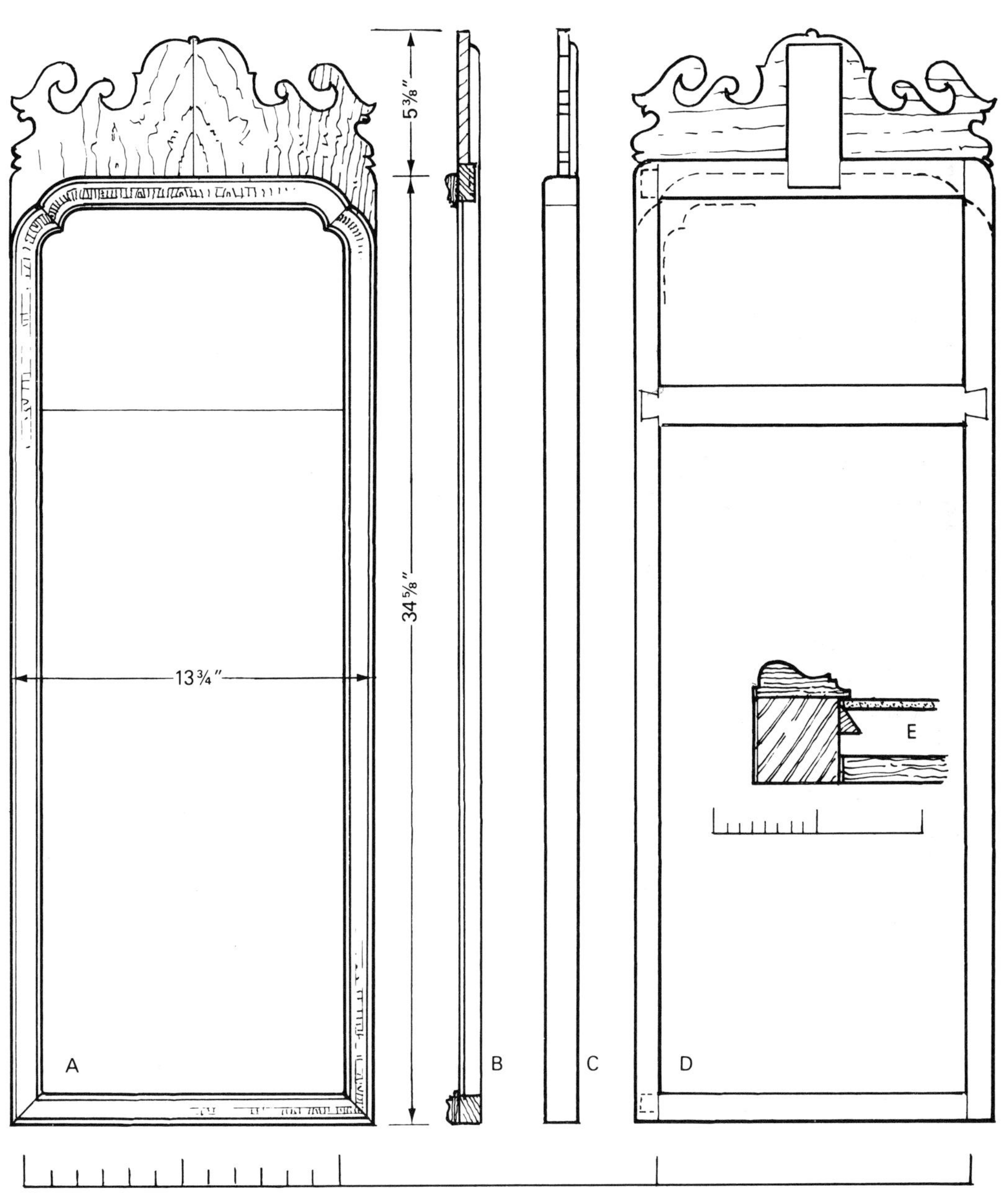

Fig. 2 **A** front elevation; **B** side section; **C** side elevation; **D** back view; **E** enlarged section through frame

Small mahogany table with slide, about 1760

A reasonable criticism of this little table is that it is more decorative than useful. It measures only some 11in. square at the top, and today would be used for little more than to hold a cup of tea, or possibly a vase. At the same time it has a delightful appearance, and would be an interesting piece to make as a reproduction. It is in mahogany throughout, except for the slide which is of oak, faced at the front with mahogany. A detail which adds considerably to the appearance is that the rails are veneered with cross-grain mahogany and the veneer is taken right over the legs.

Lightness and delicacy are essential characteristics of the table. The legs are worked in 1in. squares, and it will be realised that, as the feet

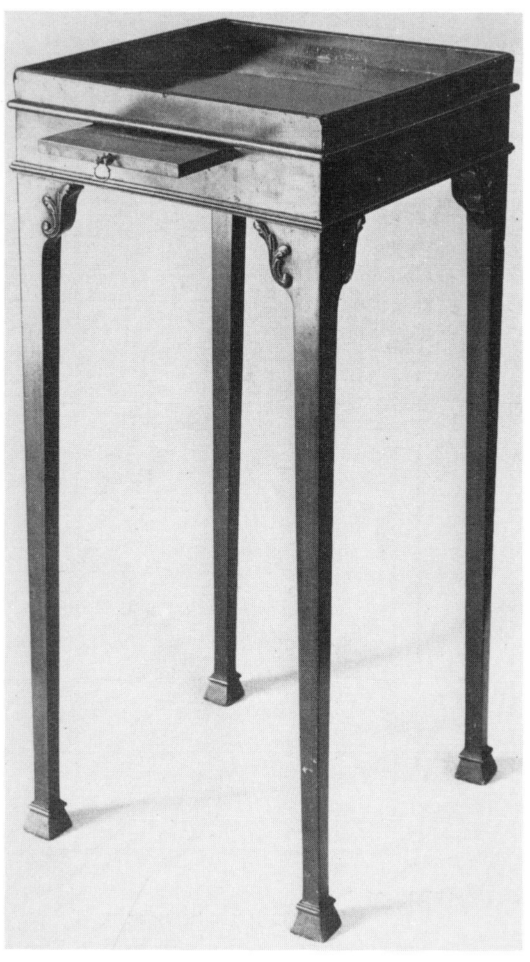

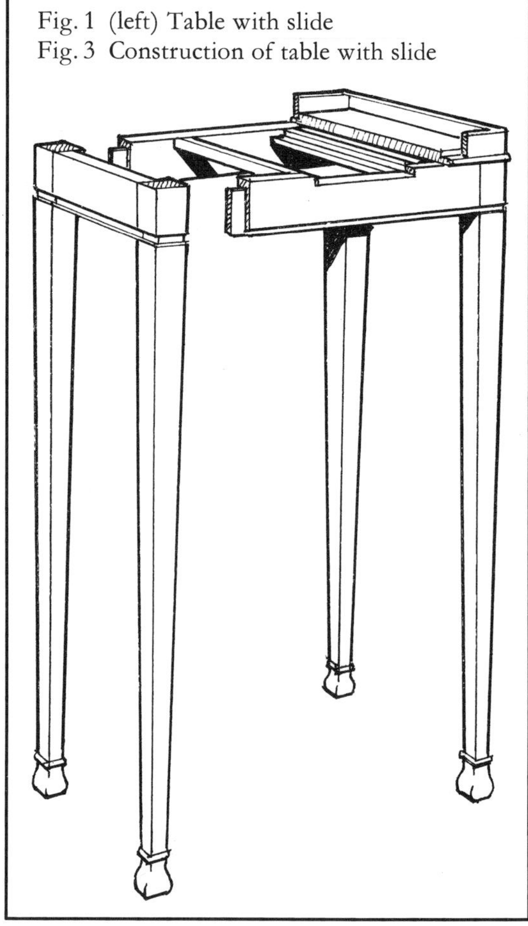

Fig. 1 (left) Table with slide
Fig. 3 Construction of table with slide

remain to the full 1in., the tapering is slightly awkward in that the plane could not be taken right through. The simplest way, having planed the stuff straight and parallel, would be to cut in a notch immediately above the foot. Two opposite sides would be worked first and the other two afterwards. In this way a short plane could be used to work the bulk of the taper, the portion adjoining the foot being completed with the bullnose plane afterwards, or possibly with the spokeshave, and finished by scraping followed by rubbing with glass-paper wrapped around a flat wood rubber. Making the feet would follow a similar process, in that opposite sides would be completed first.

The rails are tenoned into the legs, and before assembling the whole, a rebate to take the astragal moulding would be worked at the bottom edge. After being assembled, this rebate would be continued across the legs as a groove. To receive the slide, a notch is cut at the top of the front rail, and passing to the back are two rebated runners.

Resting on the framework is the top, which appears to be only $\frac{1}{4}$in. thick where it projects at the edges, but in fact it is thicker, the edges being rebated at the top to take the edging. The latter is mitred at the corners, Glue-blocks hold the top to the framework.

Drawn from the original in the possession of R. A. Salaman Esq.

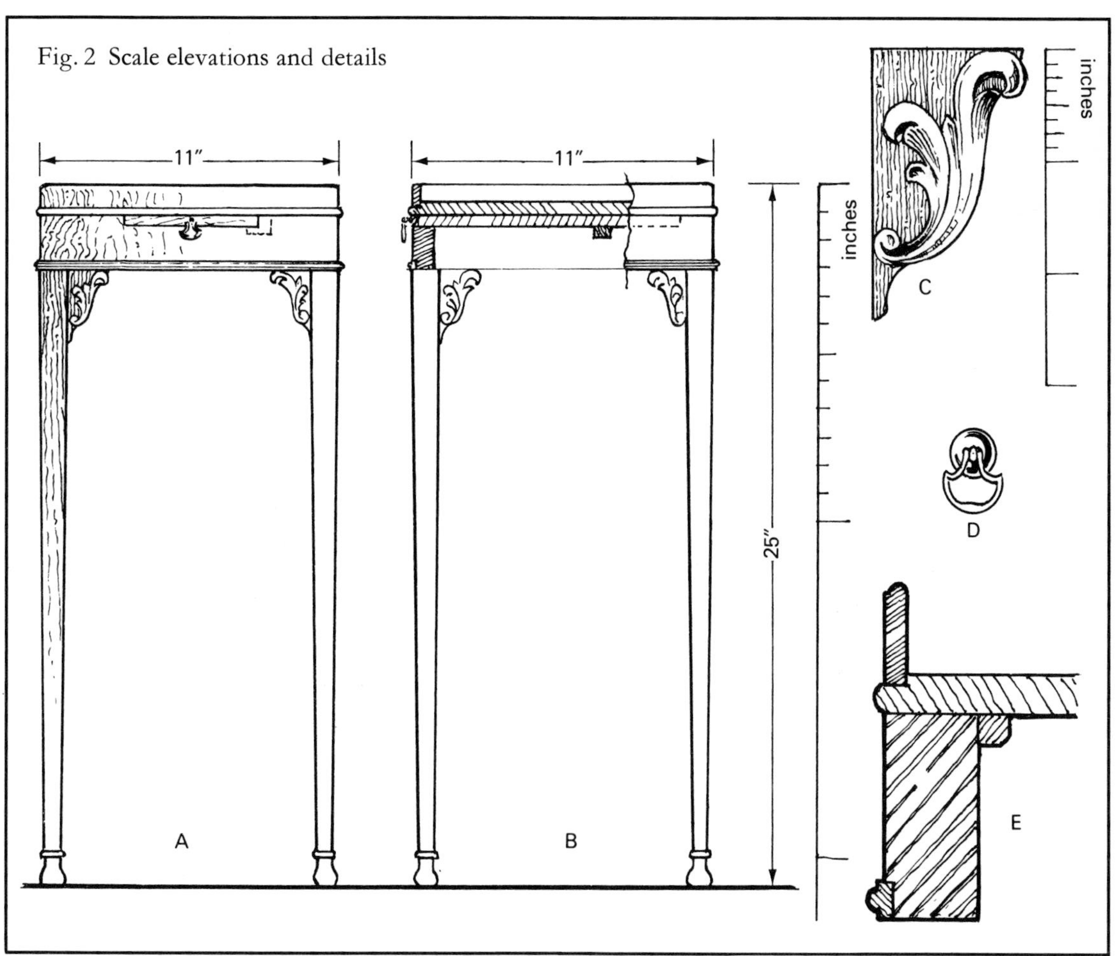

Fig. 2 Scale elevations and details

Mahogany dining table, about 1765

Fig. 1 Mahogany dining table of unusual construction,

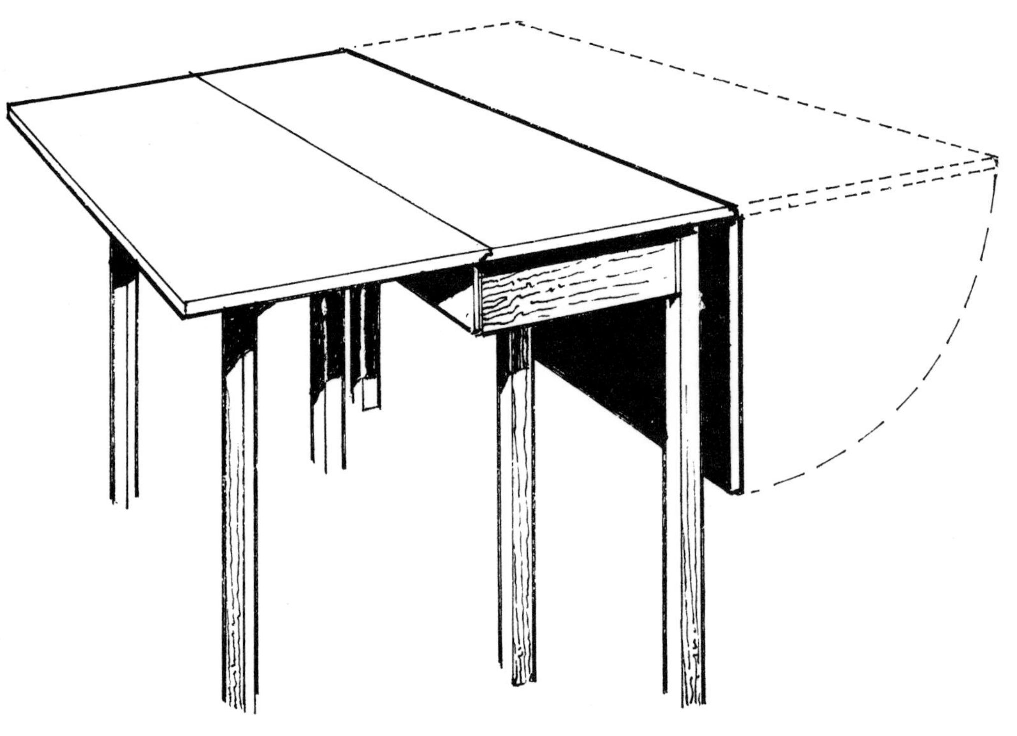

Although relatively simple, with nothing in the way of decoration, this table has an unusual form of construction, hence its inclusion in this book. It has six legs but only two of them are rigidly attached to the main framework, the others being in the form of fly legs pivoted on knuckle joints. Furthermore the fixed legs are not attached to the end rails of the framework but to two inner intermediate rails, as shown clearly in Fig. 3. This arrangement carries with it the advantage that it gives more clearance for the diners' legs beneath the top. This would particularly be the case if only one flap were raised and two diners had to sit at each end. The fixed legs if attached to the end rails would certainly be in the way. Solid Cuban mahogany was used by the maker for the tops, legs, and end rails with fly rails and concealed framework parts of beech.

The cabinet-maker realised the necessity for a really strong framework, and he secured this by lapped-dovetailing the short end rails into the long side rails, and through-tenoning the intermediate rails to hold the fixed legs. Furthermore, he provided extra stiffening by dovetailing two centre rails as in Fig. 3. To provide a sound fixing for the legs he cut shallow grooves across the rails at the outer side to resist side movement, and cut an additional tenon to fit into the underside of the rails. It will be noticed that rebates are cut at the corners of the framework to enable the fly legs and rails to close flush against the side rails, the legs being notched for the purpose as shown at C, Fig. 2. This illustration also shows the top of the knuckle joint used for the fly rails. The fixed part of this knuckle joint, X, is common to both fly rails, of course, and is screwed to the

Fig. 3 Construction of main framework

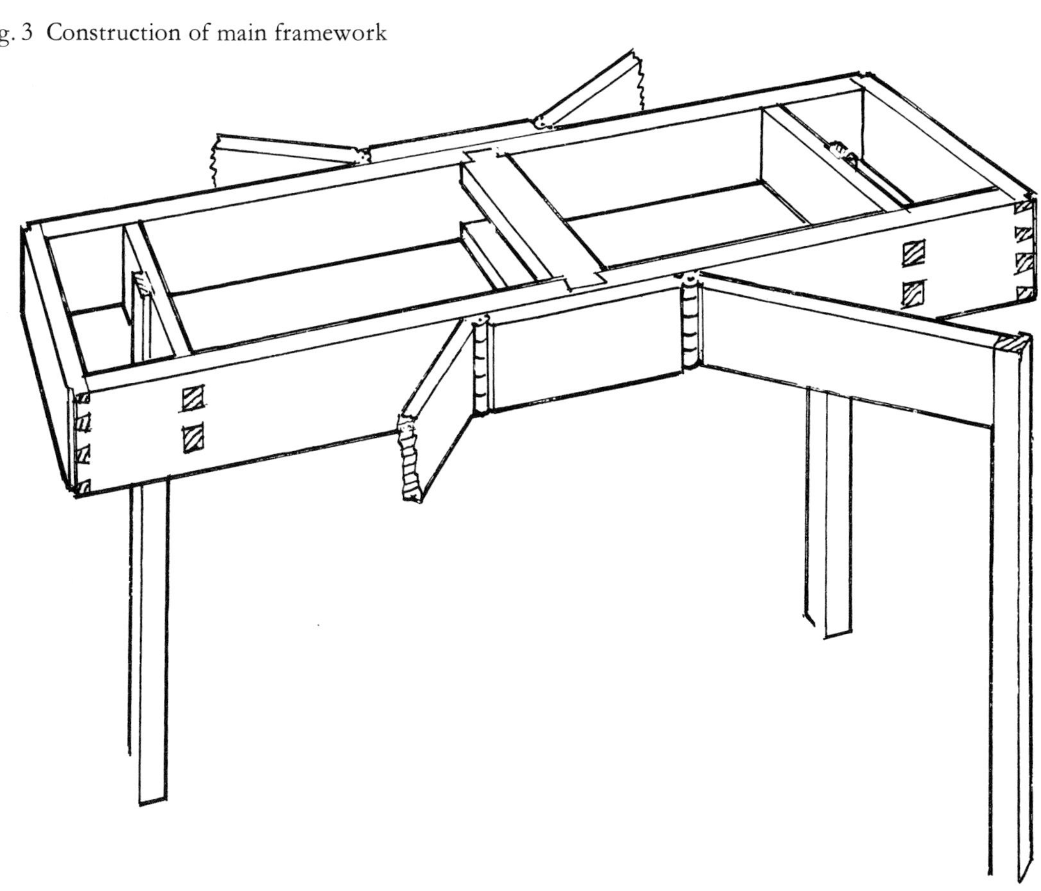

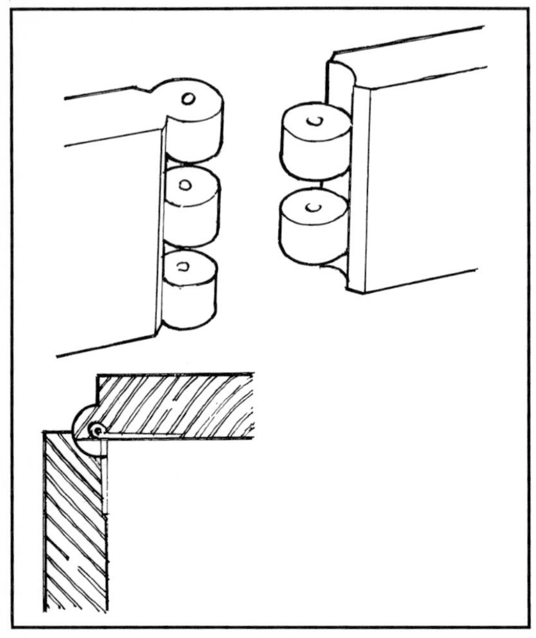

side rails. Fig. 4 shows the joint in greater detail, and it will be realised that it owes its strength not merely to the iron pin which passes through its centre, but also to the bearing surfaces which resist wear.

A rule joint is used between the flaps and the main top. In this case unusually deep squares with correspondingly reduced round and hollow members have been cut as shown in Fig. 5.

Fig. 4 (top left) Detail of knuckle joint
Fig. 5 (bottom left) Rule joint between top and flap
Fig. 2 Scale drawing of dining table. **A** front and side elevations; **B** plan; **C** joint of gate-leg

Fig. 2

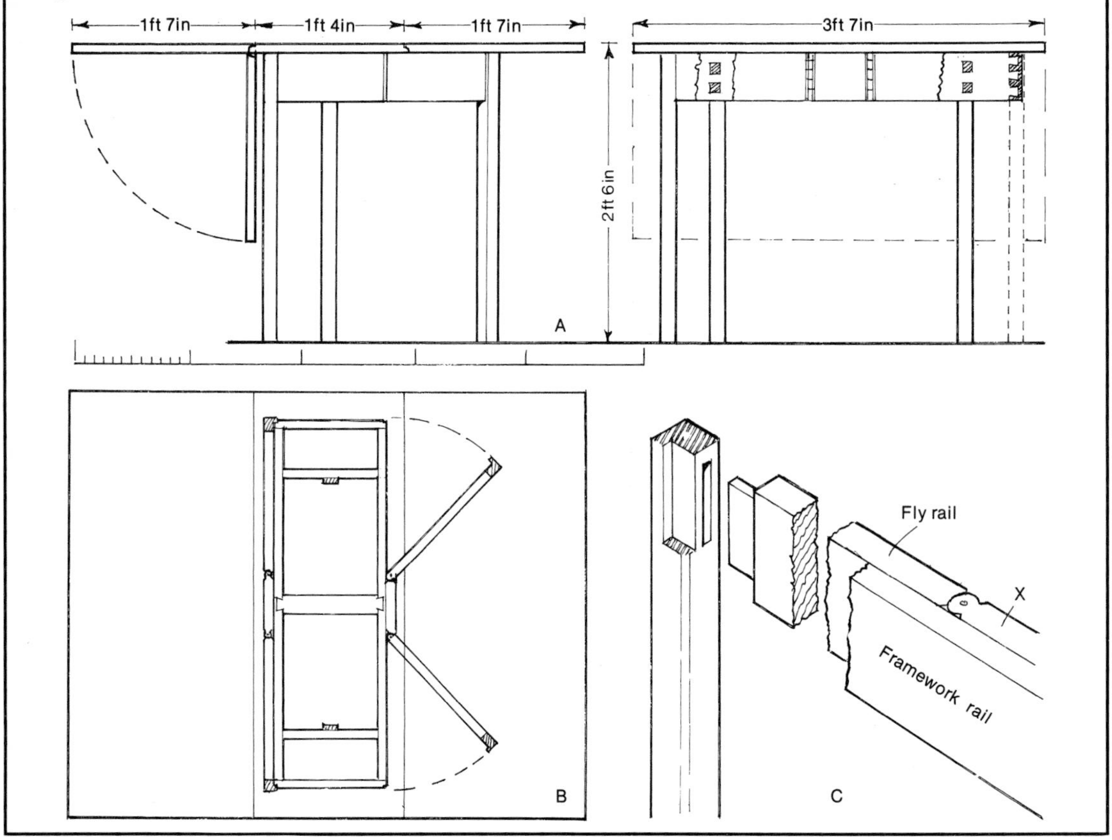

1ft 7in 1ft 4in 1ft 7in

3ft 7in

2ft 6in

A

B

Fly rail

X

Framework rail

C

Mahogany table or stand with fretted gallery, second half of the 18th century

Drawn from the original at Ascott House, Buckinghamshire.

Besides having several novel features, this delightful table has the stamp of being the product of an extremely competent designer and highly skilled cabinet-maker. It has admirable proportions, the detail is refined, and the legs are slightly splayed, giving a sense of stability. This unusual feature probably does give slight additional stability, but the likelihood is that it was appearance that the designer had chiefly in mind. An attractive feature is the bowed end of the top with correspondingly curved gallery. It was no doubt intended to accommodate an urn, leaving the rest of the space and the shelves for cups, glasses, plates, etc.

It is interesting to speculate how the whole was assembled, and the type of construction used. Since the two shaped shelves are tenoned into the chamfered inner surfaces of the legs, it is clear that normal methods of assembly could not be used. In the usual way, the two opposite top rails would be glued into their legs, and the other rails added after the glue had set. But this would have been impossible in the present case because, whereas the shelf tenons enter the legs at 45 degrees, the top tenons enter at 90 degrees. There could only have been one answer. The shelves and legs were assembled first and the top rails dropped in from above afterwards, their mortises being open at the top. It is of course impossible to see this because the top is a fixture and is held with glue-blocks beneath, but it seems to be the only method that could have been used.

Although the shelves are only $\frac{3}{8}$in. thick they are halved together as in Fig. 4 (also B, Fig. 2). It will be realised that although all four tenons are set at right angles with each other (because the leg chamfers are at 45 degrees) they are not in alignment axially with the two boards forming the halving. In practice the two pieces would be halved together at the required angle, and the tenons and curves set out and cut afterwards.

Fig. 1 Mahogany table with fretted gallery

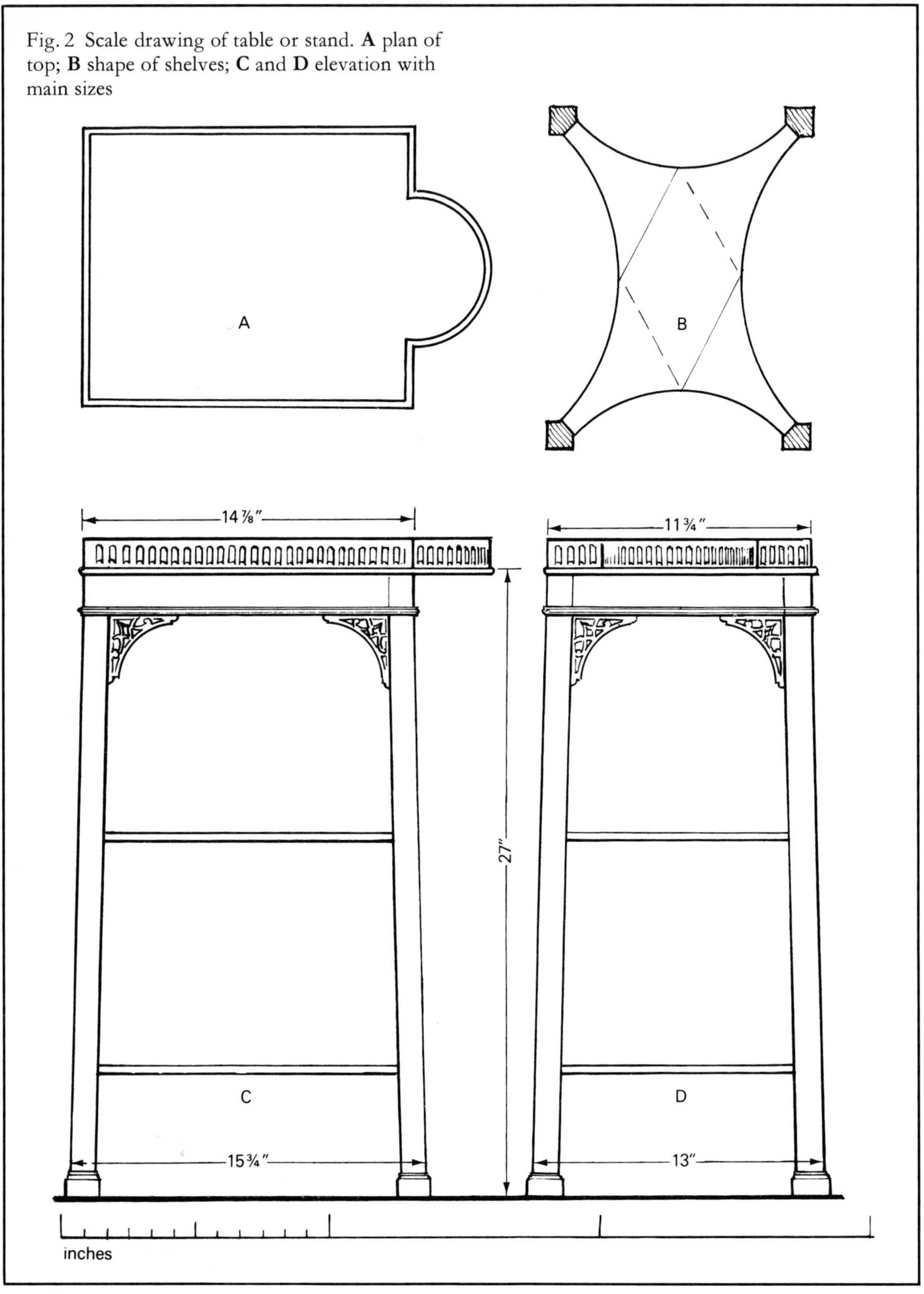

Fig. 2 Scale drawing of table or stand. **A** plan of top; **B** shape of shelves; **C** and **D** elevation with main sizes

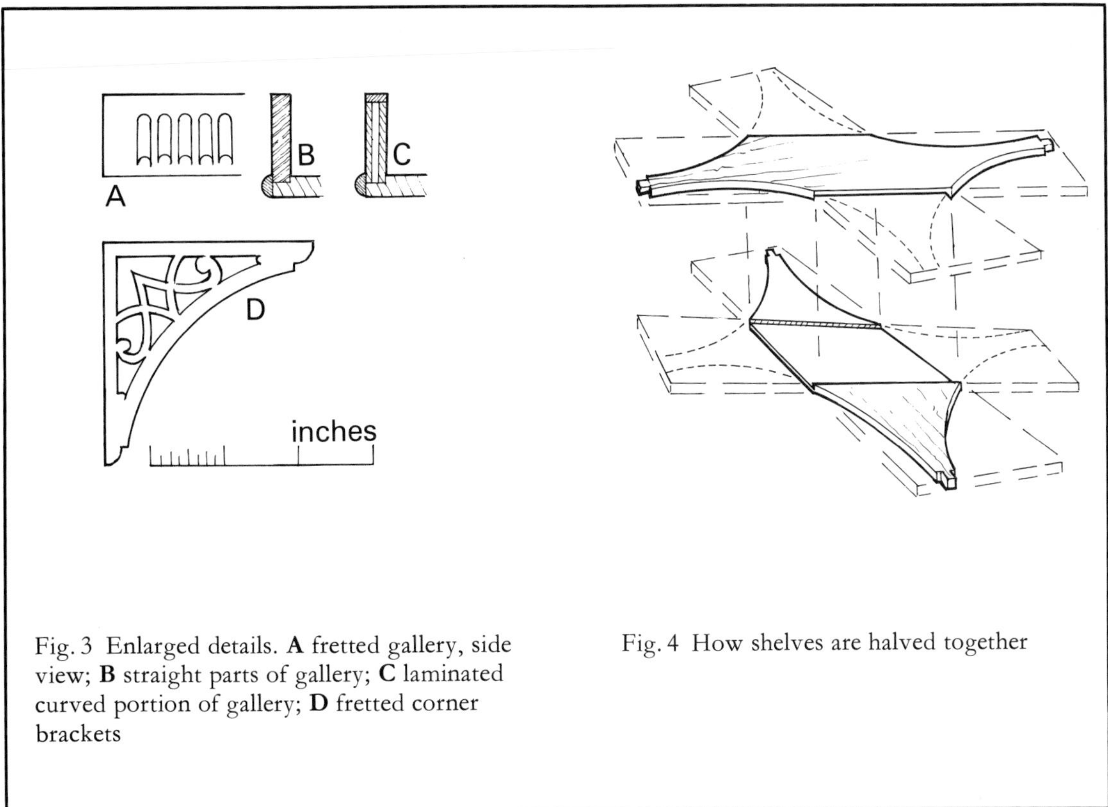

Fig. 3 Enlarged details. **A** fretted gallery, side view; **B** straight parts of gallery; **C** laminated curved portion of gallery; **D** fretted corner brackets

Fig. 4 How shelves are halved together

Since there is no taper to the legs the feet are formed by planting on moulded pieces all round, and these in fact project downwards, forming recesses in which there were originally castors (they are now missing). A $\frac{3}{8}$in. astragal moulding is fitted level with the bottom edges of the top rails and is set in a rebate, the legs being grooved so that the recess is continued to the corners. The shapes of the fretted bracket are given at D, Fig. 3. These are glued in and thin glue-blocks rubbed in to give strength.

Details of the fretted gallery are given at A, B, and C, Fig. 3. It will be seen that the top is rebated to receive the gallery and a thin half-round moulding is planted on all round. Straight portions of the gallery are in solid $\frac{1}{4}$in. stuff, but the curved portion is laminated in three thicknesses to enable it to be bent to shape. No doubt the cabinet-maker made a former or pair of formers and, having steamed the wood to make it pliable, applied cramps but used no glue. After several hours the cramps would be removed, the wood finally dried, glue applied, and the cramps again fixed. After trimming to shape, the patterns would be fretted. This would be an awkward job and the craftsman probably made a special cutting-board to support the wood whilst fretting. Note from C, Fig. 3 that a thin piece is glued at the top to hide the laminations.

It would have been necessary to steam the small half-round moulding at the bottom, and, as the radius is only 3$\frac{1}{4}$in., it may have been necessary to do the bending in two or more stages, increasing the curvature at each. It is quite likely that the cabinet-maker may have had failures before being successful, because mahogany is not the easiest wood to bend.

Mahogany bookcase-cupboard, second half of the 18th century

Fig. 1 Front and side elevations of bookcase cupboard

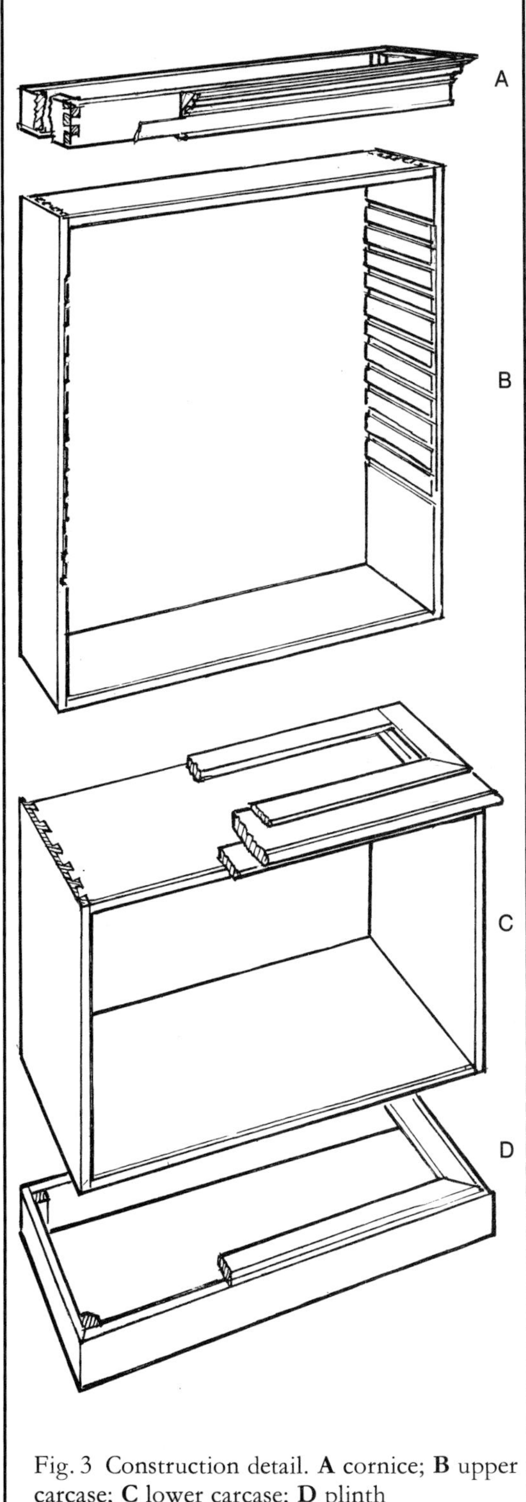

Fig. 3 Construction detail. **A** cornice; **B** upper carcase; **C** lower carcase; **D** plinth

This is a type of bookcase made in increasing numbers in the second half of the eighteenth century, and it embodies the usual constructional features of the period. It consists of two main carcases with separate cornice and plinth. All show parts are of mahogany (large surfaces veneered) with softwood concealed parts and adjustable shelves edged with mahogany.

Both upper and lower carcases are lap-dovetailed together as in Fig. 3, the tops and bottoms being of softwood with edgings of mahogany at the front. To give a neat finish to the ends when the doors are opened, a rounded moulding is worked along the front edges to line up with the trenches which hold the adjustable shelves. The backs of pieces of this kind varied widely. In the best work they were framed and panelled, but others had a plain muntin back or even plain boards with vertical rebated joints.

The traceried doors follow a pattern common in the later eighteenth century, the section of the moulding being an astragal grooved at the back to fit over the stiffening back bars as shown at E, Fig. 2. Not all such pieces had grooved mouldings, however. In many cases they were merely glued to the front edges of the bars. Glass was frequently puttied in, though in the present case beading is used (F, Fig. 2).

Construction of the lower doors is given in Fig. 5. There is a plain square-edged framework with a flush panel fitted with a bare-faced tongue as at B, Fig. 2, the veneer on the face being taken over the entire front surface. No doubt the maker kept his panel timber for a long time to ensure its being really dry, otherwise shrinkage would have caused splits which would have shown through as stress marks on the surface of the veneer. As it is, it has remained remarkably free from trouble. The maker could have applied his astragal moulding right over the joint to conceal any possible opening of the joints. Instead, he has put the moulding over the framework immediately to the side of the joint (B, Fig. 2). The small quadrant mouldings would have

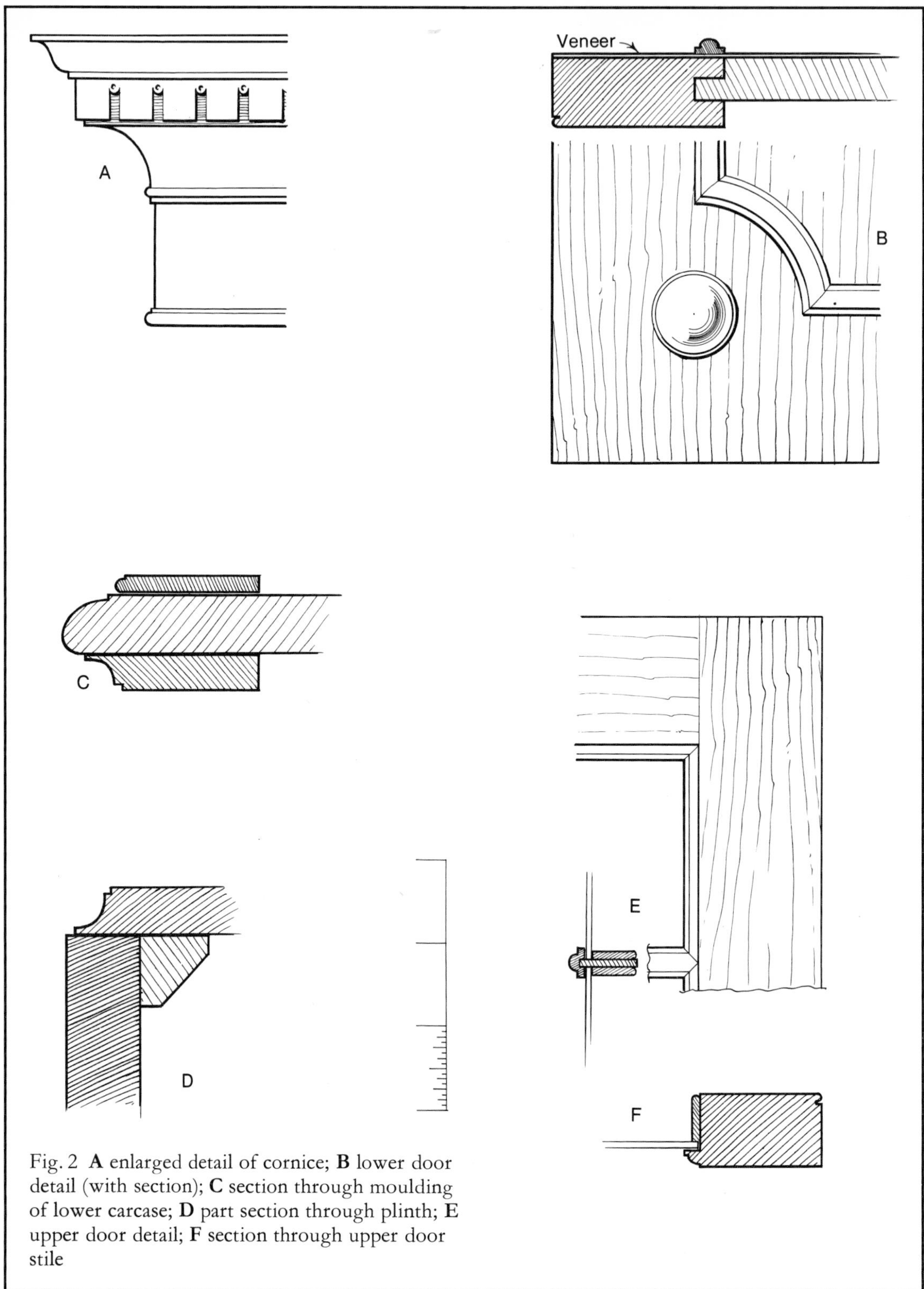

Fig. 2 **A** enlarged detail of cornice; **B** lower door detail (with section); **C** section through moulding of lower carcase; **D** part section through plinth; **E** upper door detail; **F** section through upper door stile

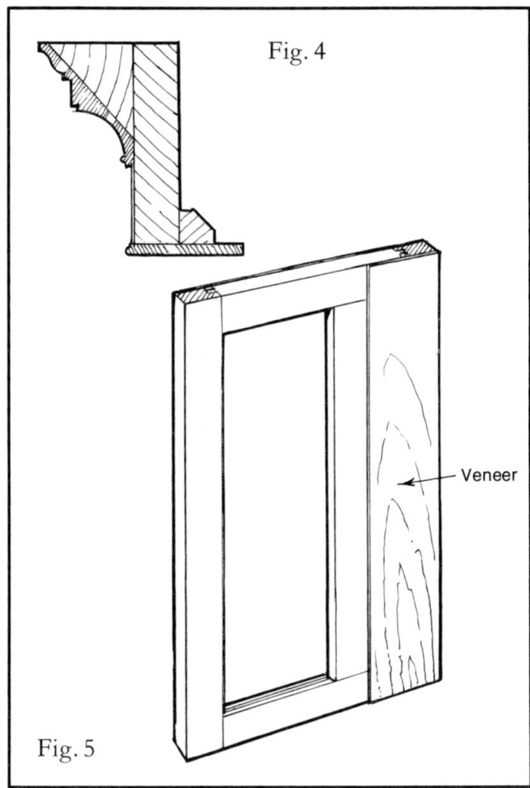

Fig. 4 Section through cornice
Fig. 5 Lower door construction

been turned on the face plate of the lathe, two complete circles being afterwards cut to form eight quarter-circles.

The plinth moulding is given at D, Fig. 2 and construction in Fig. 3. Front corners are mitred with glue blocks rubbed in at the inside, back corners being lap-dovetailed.

Fig. 3 shows the separate cornice. The advantage of making both this and the plinth as separate items is that, since the grain of the end pieces necessarily runs from front to back, they do not resist possible shrinkage of the main carcases as they would do if rigidly fixed to them. Softwood is used for the entire framework of the cornice, and the parts are dovetailed together and veneered. The cornice moulding itself is of mahogany backed with softwood (Fig. 4) and the frieze moulding is planted on beneath.

Mahogany side table, about 1780

It was largely the introduction of veneering that made possible the development of shaped work in furniture. Many years were to pass, however, before its full possibilities were realised. In the Queen Anne period, chairs with veneered shaped rails were made, but little in the way of shaped case furniture has come down to us. Sometimes large display cabinets with ogee shaped bases are found, but for the greater part the main surfaces were flat. Chippendale made occasional chests and other pieces with shaped fronts for wealthy clients, but most of his case furniture was flat.

Items that became popular in the second half of the eighteenth century were tables with bow or semi-circular fronts, the latter sometimes opening out to give a completely circular top. An example of this kind is the table in Fig. 1, which can either serve as a side table or be opened out for a meal. Today the main shaped rim would be made of several thicknesses, laminated and bent to shape round a former, a method largely made possible by the use of a machine thicknessing-planer which enables the laminae to be produced in constant thicknesses throughout. This, however, would have been an awkward (though not impossible) procedure at a time when only hand methods were available. Instead craftsmen followed what is known as the 'brick' method, a series of shaped pieces in softwood, of about 1in. thickness, being sawn out, and glued together in layers, with staggered vertical joints. These ensured strength along the length, and by having fairly short 'bricks' the presence of end grain on the surface was minimised (end grain does not hold glue well).

In the present example, the two front legs are fitted to the rim with a form of bridle joint (Fig. 4), but the rear legs are pivoted to enable them to support the top when opened. Consequently the back rail of the table is dovetailed into the ends of the semi-circular rim. Additional strength is provided by a cross rail slot-dovetailed between the back rail and the rim at the centre (Fig. 3), though in many such tables this is omitted.

Fig. 1 Semi-circular table in satinwood, opening to circular shape

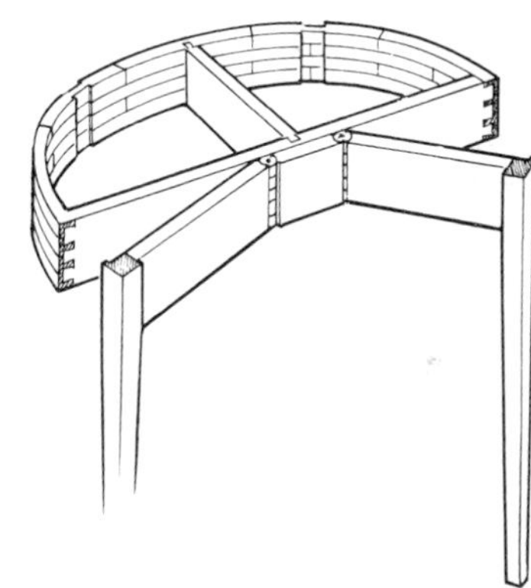

Fig. 3 Rear view showing rim construction and hingeing of back legs

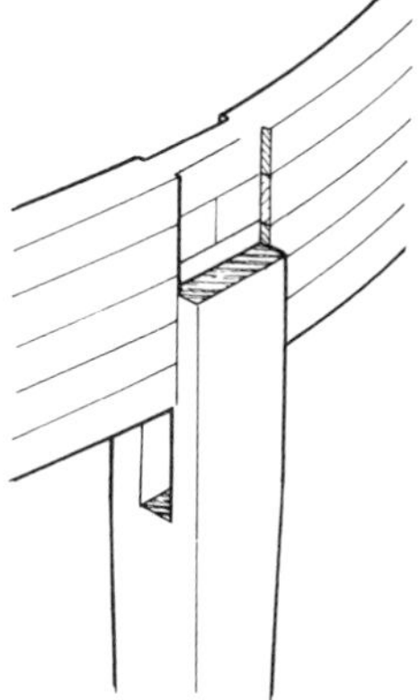

Fig. 4 Bridle joint fixing leg to rim

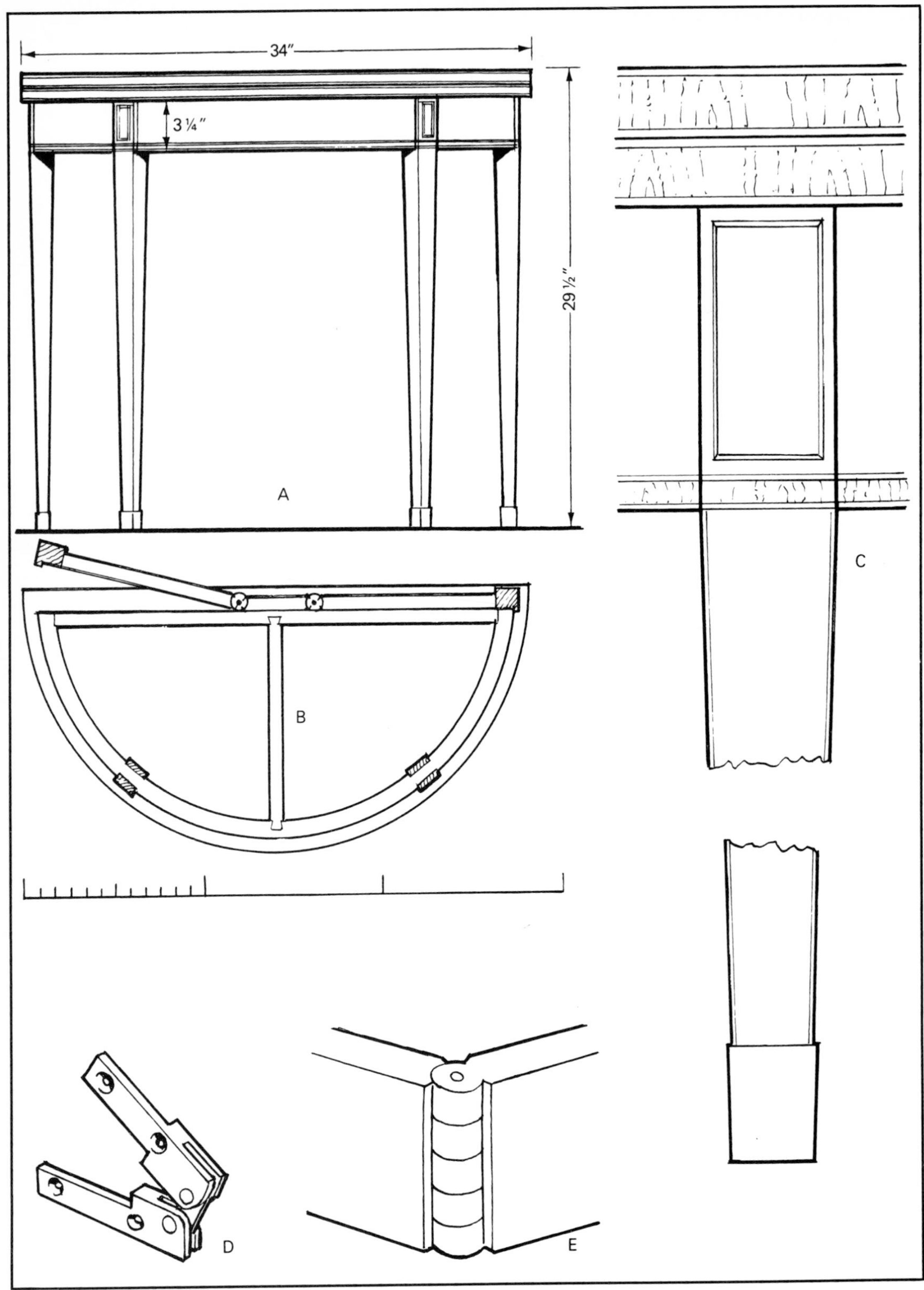
34"
3 ¼"
29 ½"
A
B
C
D
E

Fig. 2 (left) Dimensional elevation and plan. **A** front elevation; **B** plan showing back leg movement; **C** enlarged detail of leg; **D** card table hinges; **E** knuckle joint used for back legs

To enable the back legs to be pivoted, knuckle joints have been used. This joint had been introduced and perfected during the late seventeenth century, and was a common form of hinged joint for movable legs during the whole of the eighteenth century. It was a strong and reliable form of mechanical joint, carried out entirely in wood except for the centre pivot which was of iron. Its great advantage was its many bearing surfaces which resisted wear, though it can be an awkward item to repair if badly worn, or if it has been attacked by the furniture beetle (and many of them have been).

The joint is shown in detail at E, Fig. 2. Since both legs are pivoted, there is a central fixed piece screwed to the centre of the back rail, in which one part of each joint is cut.

Around both edges of the top are inlaid boxwood lines and, in addition to being a decorative detail, they protect the edges of the veneer, especially the cross-grain at the edges. The legs, too, have inlaid boxwood lines at the corners (see C, Fig. 2). Another decorative feature is the inlaid banding around the lower edge of the shaped rim and the small inlaid panels at the top of the legs. An unusual feature is that the feet are formed by little pieces of satinwood veneer glued on around all four sides. Such feet were usually cut in the solid wood, but the present method was much quicker and easier, because in tapering the legs, the plane could be taken right through, instead of having to be stopped at the projecting foot. On the other hand the veneer was in a vulnerable position and liable to be chipped off (this has actually happened in one case).

To avoid having projecting hinge knuckles at the top, when opened, special card-table hinges were used at the ends, these having double throw by virtue of the link joining the two parts of the hinge, as at D, Fig. 2.

Occasional table, about 1780

Fig. 1 Mahogany occasional table of remarkable delicacy and unusual construction

Drawn from the original in the possession of Phillips of Hitchin (Antiques) Limited.

The designer of this table must have had firm ideas of lightness and elegance, and at the same time had a remarkable capacity for designing fine detail. For instance, the legs are one of the finest examples of turning I have ever come across. They measure no more than $1\frac{3}{8}$in. at the fullest member, yet they are a remarkable example of economy in material combined with rich detail. Going with this is a most unusual form of construction, which must have given the maker a severe test of his ingenuity. In most similar tables, a square is left at the top of the legs, into which the top rails are jointed. Here, the entire leg is turned from top to bottom, making any form of direct jointing with the rails impossible. If the maker did not design the table himself, he probably had some unkind things to say about the designer, though in fact he solved the problem remarkably well.

The measurements of the table are given in the scale drawings in Fig. 2, and enlarged detail of the legs and turned stretchers in Fig. 3. Construction is shown in Fig. 4, from which it will be seen that the top framing is a sort of open box, the front rails probably dovetailed into the sides as shown. It is impossible to be sure of this without removing the top. On the underside, a wide rail ($5\frac{3}{4}$in. by $\frac{7}{16}$in.) covers whatever joints there may be. To the sides are attached thick rails, which stand in at front and back, leaving $1\frac{3}{8}$in. open corners into which the turned legs are fitted. To provide a fixing for the legs, screw-plates are used as at B, Fig. 4. This is the only example of such construction I have ever come across.

Details of the leg turning are given in Fig. 3. It should be noted that a plain member is turned level with the bottom of the rails so that screw-plates can be driven in. Towards the bottom, the bulbous member gives sufficient thickness for the stretchers to be bored in. Along the length of the plain tapered portion and the bulbous member are reeds (thirteen in all). To

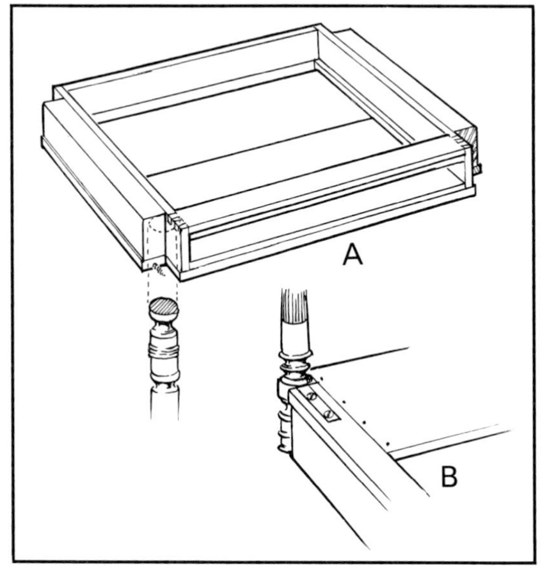

enable the straight reeds to be worked, the scratch-stock must have been used in combination with a moulding box, as shown in Fig. 5. Since the leg is tapered, it is obvious that the reeds themselves have to be tapered, so a cutter of the exact reverse shape could not be used. Instead, a pointed cutter with hollow sides would have been used to form the recesses between the reeds, and each individual reed would have been finished afterwards with glasspaper wrapped around a hollow wood

Fig. 2 (below) **A** plan in part section; **B** dovetailing of drawers; **C** front elevation; **D** side section; **E** side elevation
Fig. 4 (left) **A** how main box is made; **B** table turned upside-down showing how leg is fixed to main box with screwplates

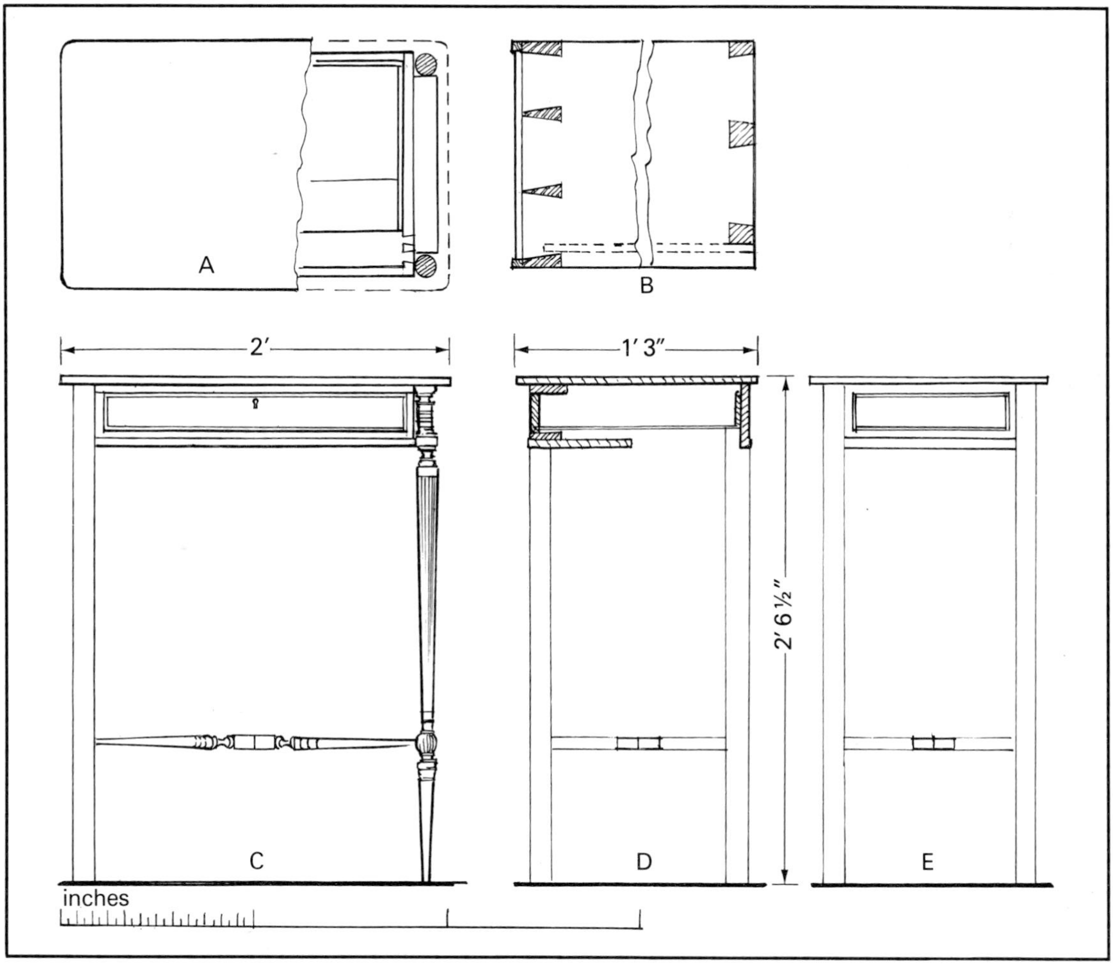

A
B
2′
1′ 3″
2′ 6½″
C
D
E
inches

rubber. Care must have been taken to stop the reeds at both ends, and it is likely that all were stopped well short of the line and finished by the carver. In any case, the bulbous member near the bottom would have been cut entirely by the carver.

The stretchers are even more delicate than the legs, and must have needed the use of a steady in the lathe, especially as the hollows near the middle are quite deep, and would have made the wood liable to bend or bounce as it revolved. The squares where the stretchers intersect are halved together.

There is nothing special about the drawer construction. Fine lapped-dovetails are used at the front, and through-dovetails at the rear, as shown at B, Fig. 2. The bottom is grooved in, with the grain running from side to side. Around the front is a $\frac{1}{8}$in. square member let into a rebate, but standing slightly proud at the front.

Fig. 3 Enlarged detail of turned leg and stretchers. **A** leg; **B** section through leg; **C** stretchers
Fig. 5 Moulding box used to work reeds in leg

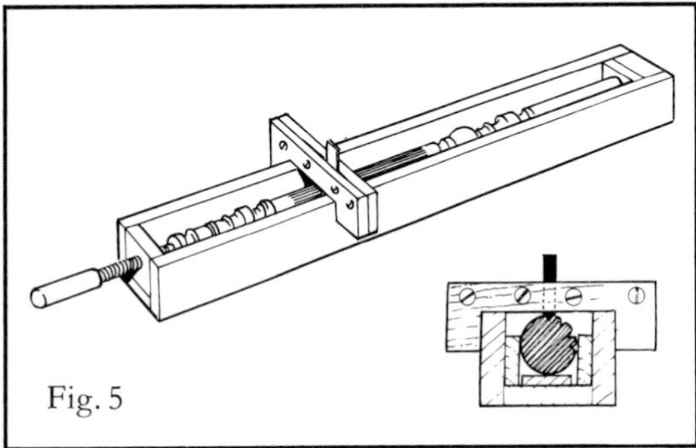
Fig. 5

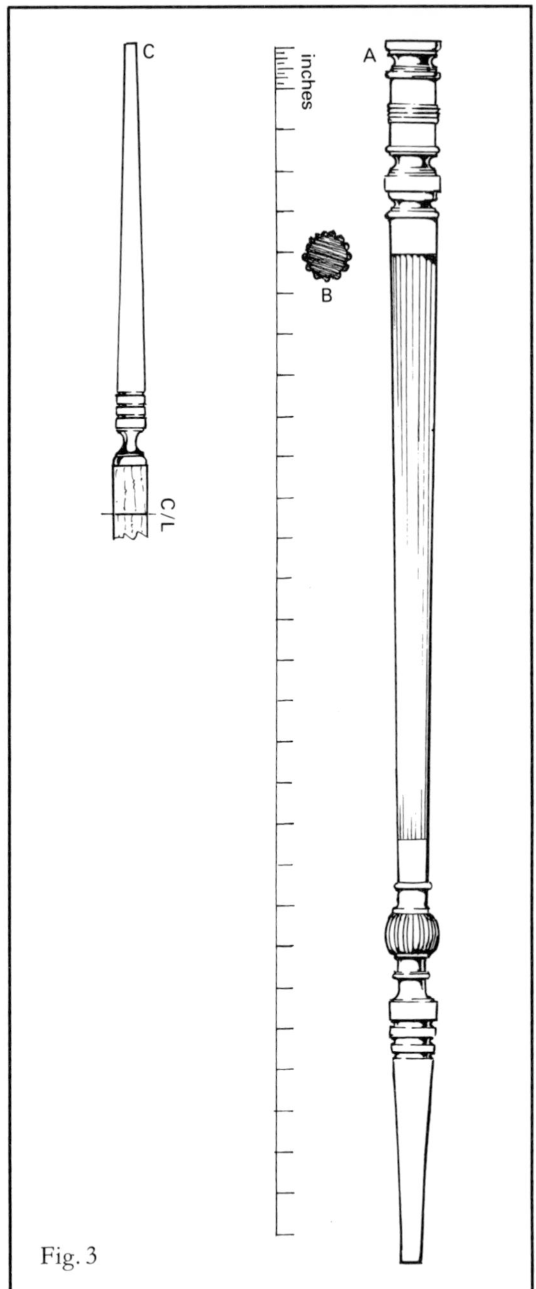

Fig. 3

Tripod reading table, late 18th century

Drawn from the original at Blickling Hall, Norfolk.

This delightful table has movements not often found in similar tripod tables. To enable it to support a book at a convenient angle, the top is made to tilt, its position being fixed by a quadrant stay pierced with holes through which a small metal pin (held on a chain) is passed. When the top is horizontal a brass table-catch holds it. Height adjustment is made by a square-sectioned rod which passed through the turned pillar; a brass knob at the top enables a pin to be passed into any one of a series of holes in a brass strip fitted flush into the square rod. To prevent the book from slipping down from the tilted top, two small brass stops are let into the lower edge. These are pivoted so that they can be pressed down flush when the top is horizontal.

Fig. 2 shows the main construction details, and it will be realised that the maker had to solve at least one awkward problem. Since the movable rod is square in section, a square hole was

Fig. 1 Tripod reading table with tilting top adjustable to height

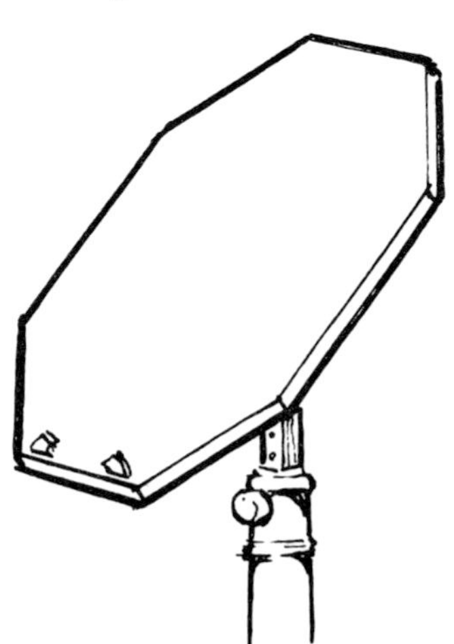

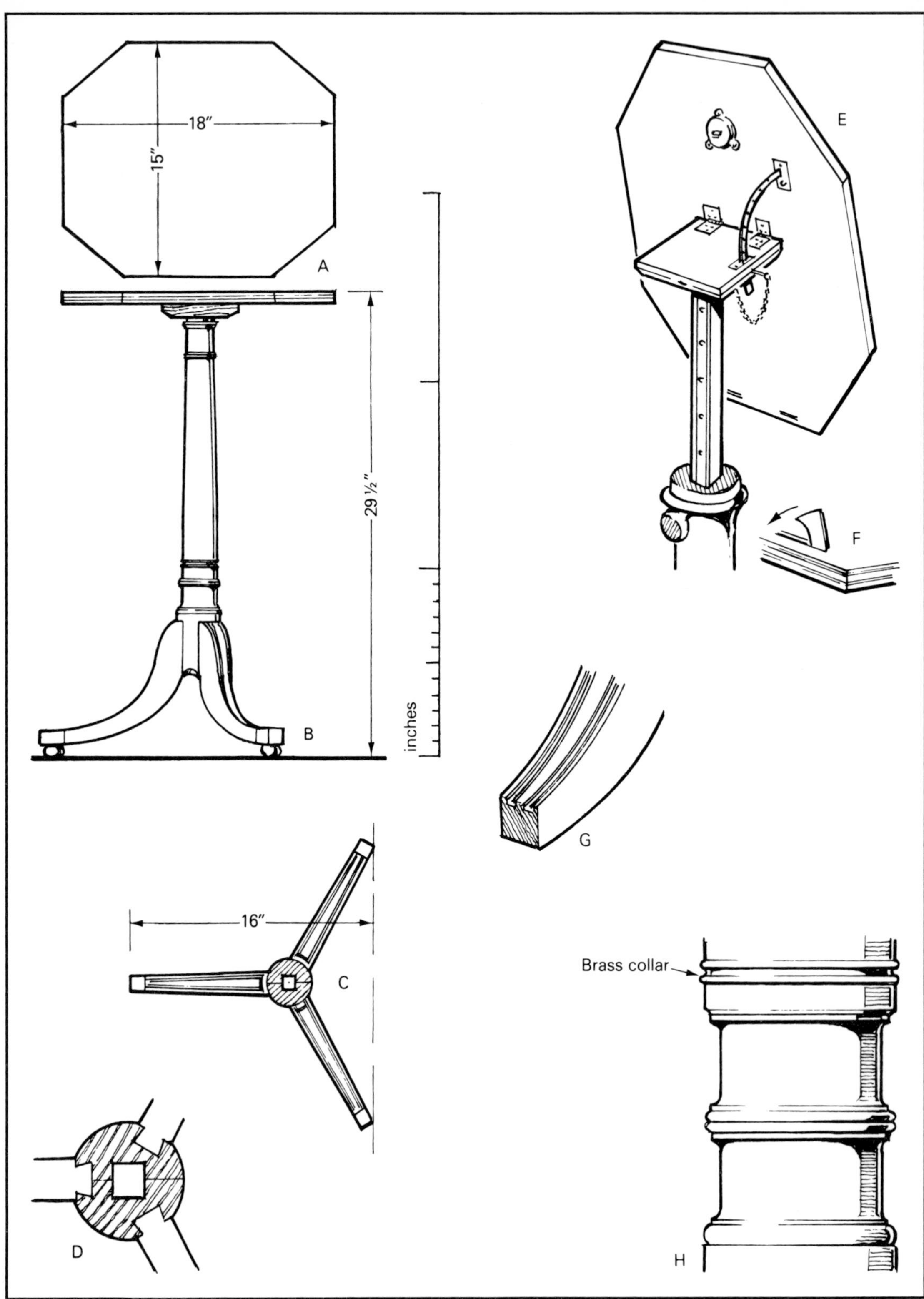
18″
15″
A
29 ½″
B
inches
E
F
G
16″
C
D
Brass collar
H

Fig. 2 (left) Details of tripod table. **A** plan of top; **B** elevation; **C** plan showing leg spread; **D** underside of pillars showing leg dovetails; **E** how top is pivoted and raised; **F** brass rest for book; **G** cut-away view of leg showing metal inlay; **H** lower part of pillar

needed in the pillar to take it. To cut a square hole right through the pillar was impossible. No woodworking tool could do it, and obviously it could not be bored on the lathe. This left only one possibility; the wood for the pillar had to be in two pieces so that a square groove $\frac{3}{8}$in. deep could be cut with the plough plane in each. They were then glued together, and the pillar turned. In a quality piece of this kind, however, it was desirable to hide the fact that the pillar was jointed, and the maker therefore sawed the wood for the pillar down the centre, planed a perfect joint, ploughed his grooves, and then turned it. In this way the joint did not show because the grain was continuous across the joint and matched perfectly. He realised however that the joint would necessarily be subjected to a certain amount of strain, and he therefore arranged to fit a circular brass collar at the top and a similar ring lower down.

The tripod legs are slot-dovetailed in the usual way, as at D, Fig. 2, and on the upper curved surface is a moulded brass inlay parallel with the sides, as at G. The feet are small brass turned knobs. The adjustment mechanism is shown at E. To one side of the small square block at the top of the square rod are two back-flap hinges which enable the top to be tilted, and the table-top catch holds the top when flat. A slot in the square block enables the quadrant to pass through. A chain holds the pin which passes through the quadrant. The same illustration shows how a knob at the top of the pillar controls a pin which engages with the holes at the side of the square rod.

Lastly the small brass stops which hold the book are a friction fit in slots at one edge, as at F. They need merely to be pushed up or down, as required.

Late 18th-century sideboard

Photograph of the original in the possession of R.A. Salaman Esq.

Sideboards made towards the end of the eighteenth century were by and large of a general type, though they varied in detail. That in Fig. 1 is typical and is included because, in addition to exemplifying a construction found in most such pieces, it has certain details which may cause some speculation as to how they were carried out. Perhaps the chief way in which these sideboards varied was in plan shape, and Fig. 2 shows some of the favourite shapes. Many other shapes appear in the published books of the late eighteenth century.

Of those shown, that at C is the most complicated and difficult to make, and consequently the most expensive. If one refers to page 94 the construction of the bow-front sideboard is given. This is typical but a little reflection shows that it could not apply in its entirety to the serpentine front with shaped ends given at C, Fig. 2. Since the ends curve outwards at the front in a similar curve to that

Fig. 1 Bow-fronted sideboard

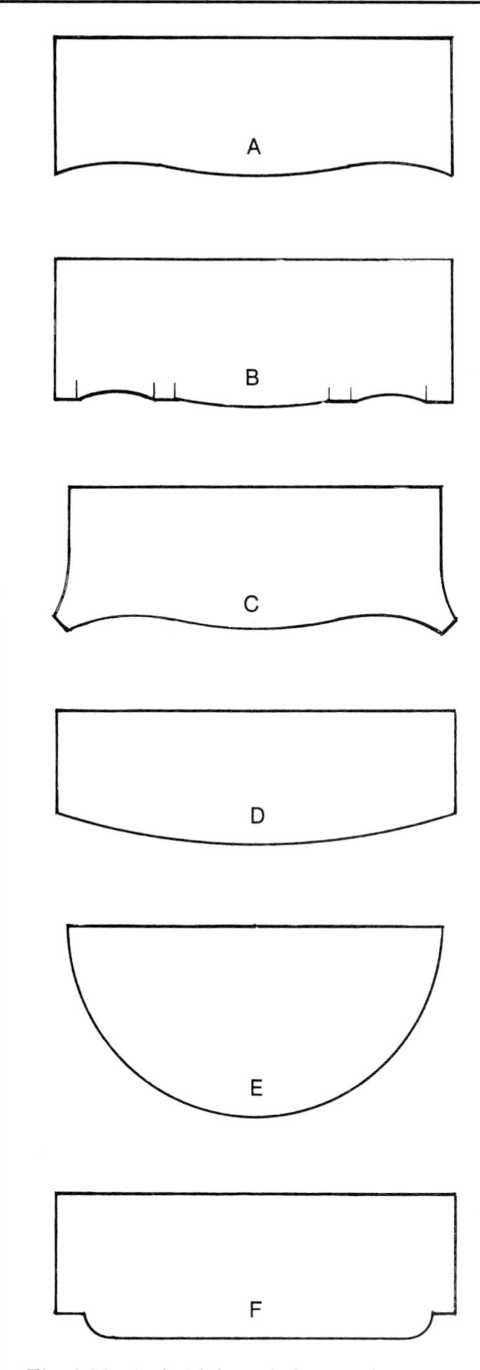

Fig. 2 Typical sideboard shapes. **A** serpentine; **B** broken serpentine front; **C** serpentine with shaped ends; **D** bow-front; **E** semicircular (sometimes semi-elliptical); **F** flat front with shaped ends

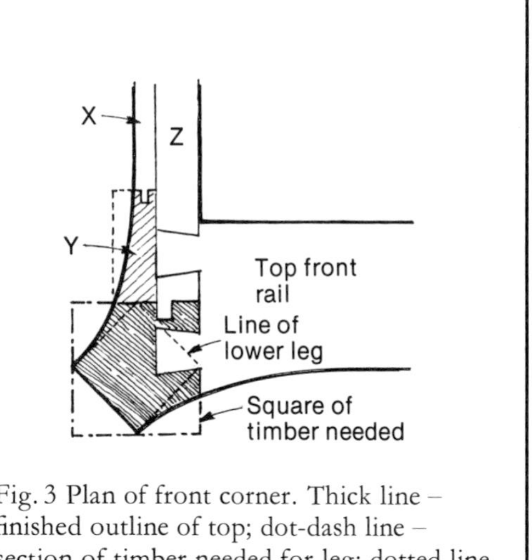

Fig. 3 Plan of front corner. Thick line – finished outline of top; dot-dash line – section of timber needed for leg; dotted line – section at lower leg.

of the front it is clear that the end leg must be set at an angle of 45 degrees, but it is not practicable to use a normal square of wood for the purpose because it would be extremely difficult if not impossible to make a strong joint. Furthermore, the edges of the upper part would have to be square with the general line of the front to enable the drawers to run properly and also to give a suitable surface to which the ends could be jointed.

Construction depends to an extent upon the degree of curvature of the front, and whether the leg is required to show the same thickness at the corner, and this involves a rather large section of timber. Note from Fig. 3 that the two inner surfaces are at right angles, thus providing a square surface against which the drawer can run, and simplifying the joints. Two rails tenoned in at each side provide the main strength, and these are barefaced to enable them to be set well in from the surface. The top rail tenon is also set well down from the top so that the front dovetail of the rail does not cut it away. Only the haunch appears at the top as shown. The panel X is merely a form of filling with piece Y tongued on to enable the curve to be worked. The dotted line shows the section before working the curve. Beneath the drawer

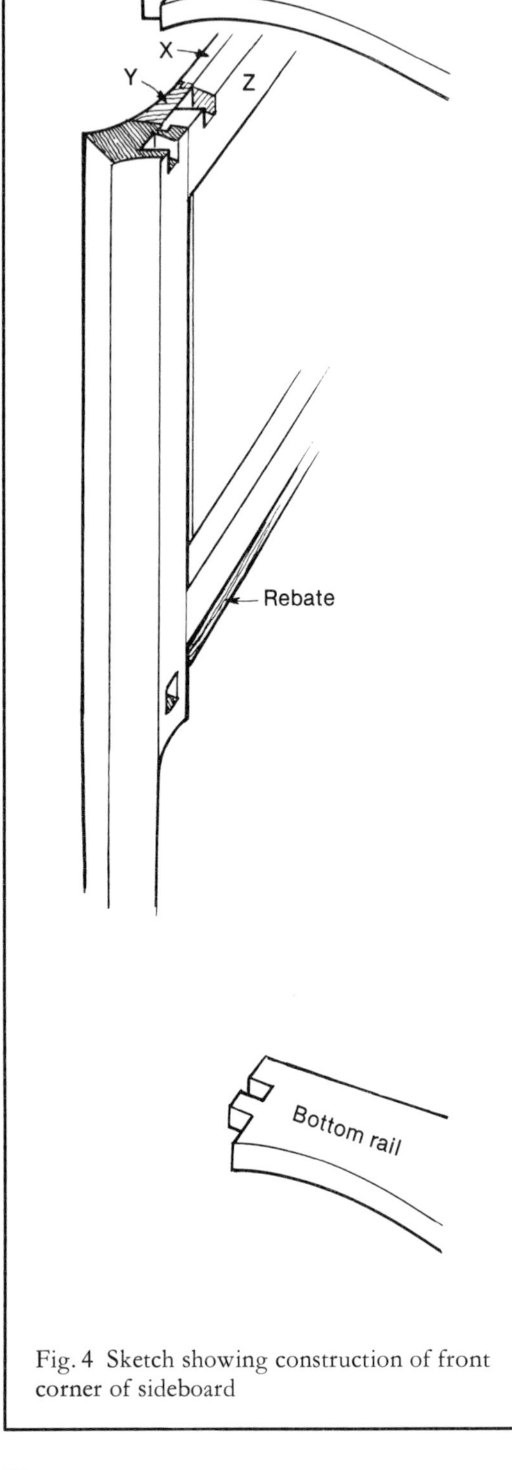

Fig. 4 Sketch showing construction of front corner of sideboard

rail the leg is square in section, but a small hollow curve is cut to enable the pointed upper corner to flow into the back of the leg. This is shown in Fig. 4.

Reverting to the sideboard in Fig. 1, it will be seen that each side drawer has a circular cross-banding inlaid into the veneer (Fig. 5), and it is obvious that the craftsman had to make this up specially for the purpose. First the groove to receive it had to be cut and for this a radius rod with cutter had to be used, as shown in Fig. 6. A nail or screw was driven in near one end and was used as a pivot (the drawer handle later hid the hole), and a cutter, fixed at the other end, cut the two sides of the groove. This enabled the veneer between the two cuts to be lifted away, a narrow hot iron being used to heat the glue and so soften it, though some craftsmen may have preferred to do the work immediately after veneering so that the waste strip could be lifted away before the glue had set.

To make the shaped banding, a large number of curved cross-grained pieces of veneer was required, and the same general idea as for the grooving was used. The object was to make the veneer pieces so that no trimming was required. The pivoting nail was driven into a flat board on which the veneer was placed, Fig. 7. The two knives shown were held in position with screws and their distance apart had to be less than the groove width to allow for the boxwood line at each side. After each cut either the veneer or the pivot was shifted to enable another cut to be made.

To enable the banding to be assembled a thin wood disc was cut out, and one boxwood line fitted up to it as in Fig. 8. Today little strips of gummed tape would be used to hold it, but at the time this sideboard was made small nails would have been knocked in at the outside to prevent the line from springing away. Up to this line the curved pieces of cross-grained veneer were fitted, the joints between each being cut radially. This is shown in Fig. 9. Finally the outer boxwood line was fitted in the same way.

It will be realised that to make up the complete circle to fit exactly into the groove would not be easy. The slightest discrepancy would make it impossible to fit into the groove. The trick was to make the banding slightly oversize. It was then cut through and the ends trimmed so that by compressing the circle it made a close fit in the groove. It was then glued in position and pressed down with the cross-peen of the hammer.

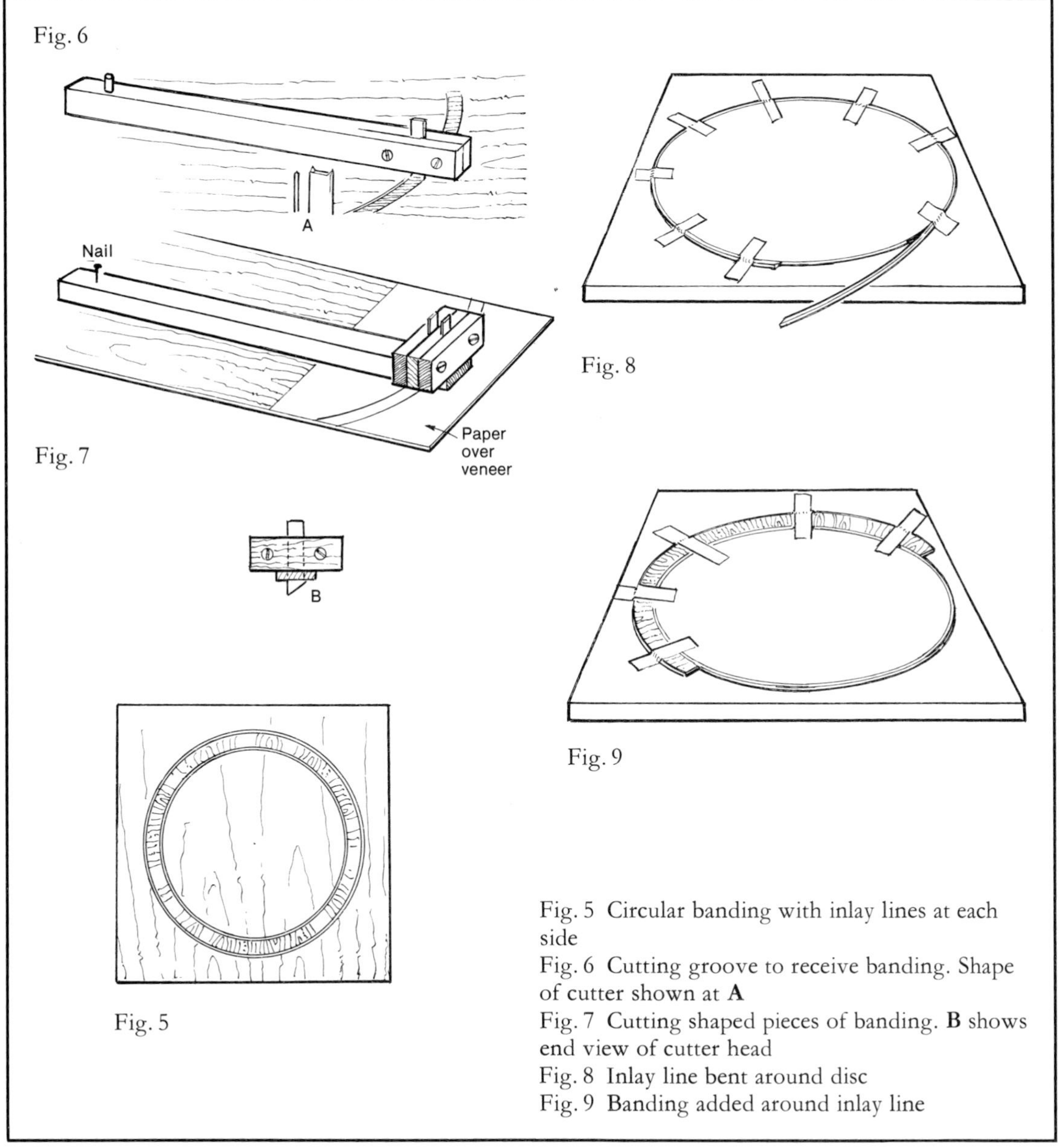

Fig. 5 Circular banding with inlay lines at each side
Fig. 6 Cutting groove to receive banding. Shape of cutter shown at **A**
Fig. 7 Cutting shaped pieces of banding. **B** shows end view of cutter head
Fig. 8 Inlay line bent around disc
Fig. 9 Banding added around inlay line

Satinwood Pembroke table, late 18th century

Drawn from the original in possession of R. A. Salaman Esq.

Many tables of this kind are illustrated in Hepplewhite's *The Cabinet Maker and Upholsterer's Guide*, and in Sheraton's *The Cabinet Maker and Upholsterer's Drawing Book*. Sheraton in fact calls it 'a kind of breakfast table from the name of the lady who first gave orders for one of them'. Many of them have extremely fine inlay and marquetry decoration and most of them are exceptionally well proportioned, light and delicate yet surprisingly robust. All have two flaps supported by brackets when extended, usually with a drawer at one end and sometimes at both ends. A common shape for the top was an ellipse, but variations were a plain oblong (possibly with the corners taken off), or a serpentine shape, or straight sides with bowed ends. Just why a small table of this kind was specially suitable for breakfast is not clear, but probably the purpose was simply that of an occasional table, which would take up little space when not in use, but would be handy for a light meal or drink of some sort in the drawing-room.

Fig. 2 Front and side elevations and plan partly cut away to show framework. **A** section through rule joint of top; **B** detail of top inlay

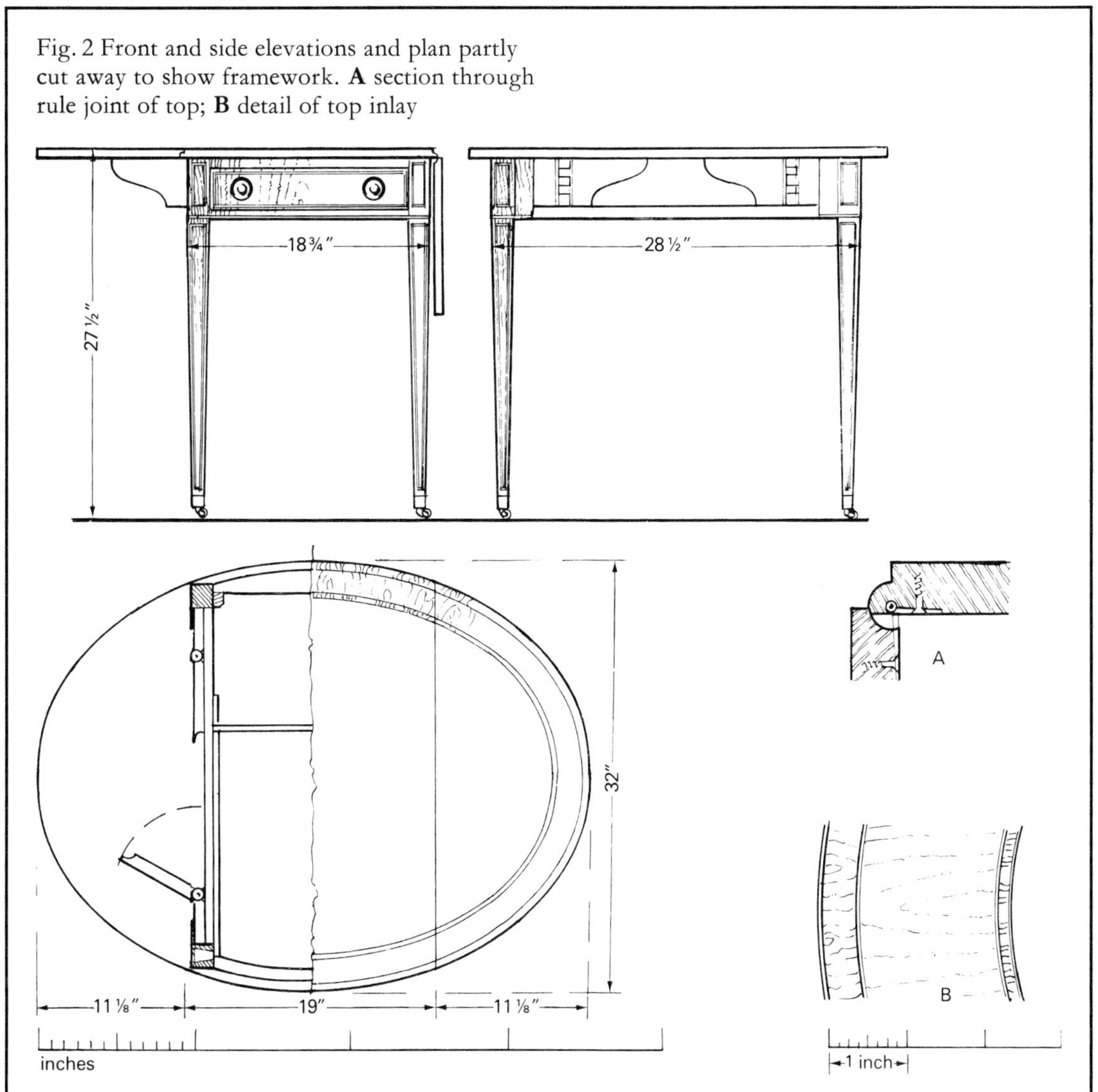

Fig. 1 Satinwood Pembroke table

In the table in Fig. 1, the legs are in solid satinwood, but other parts – top, rails and drawer fronts – are in oak, veneered with satinwood. At one end is a curved rail in the form of a dummy drawer front tenoned into the legs. There are two flat rails at the other end, the top one dovetailed in, and the other tenoned. It will be seen from Fig. 2 that the maker has fitted the side rails flush with the inside of the legs, to provide continuous side surfaces against which the drawer could run. These rails, however, reach down only to the top of the lower end rail, and he has planted on wide strips beneath which act as runners (see X, Fig. 3). They project at the outside also and form a seating for the hinged brackets which support the flaps when opened. The fixed parts of the brackets are probably tenoned into the legs to provide additional strength, as the side rails are $\frac{5}{8}$in. thick only. Since the brackets are $\frac{7}{8}$in. thick and have to stand in about $\frac{3}{16}$in. at the outside it is clear that the main rails could be no more than $\frac{5}{8}$in. thick. Kickers are glued on at

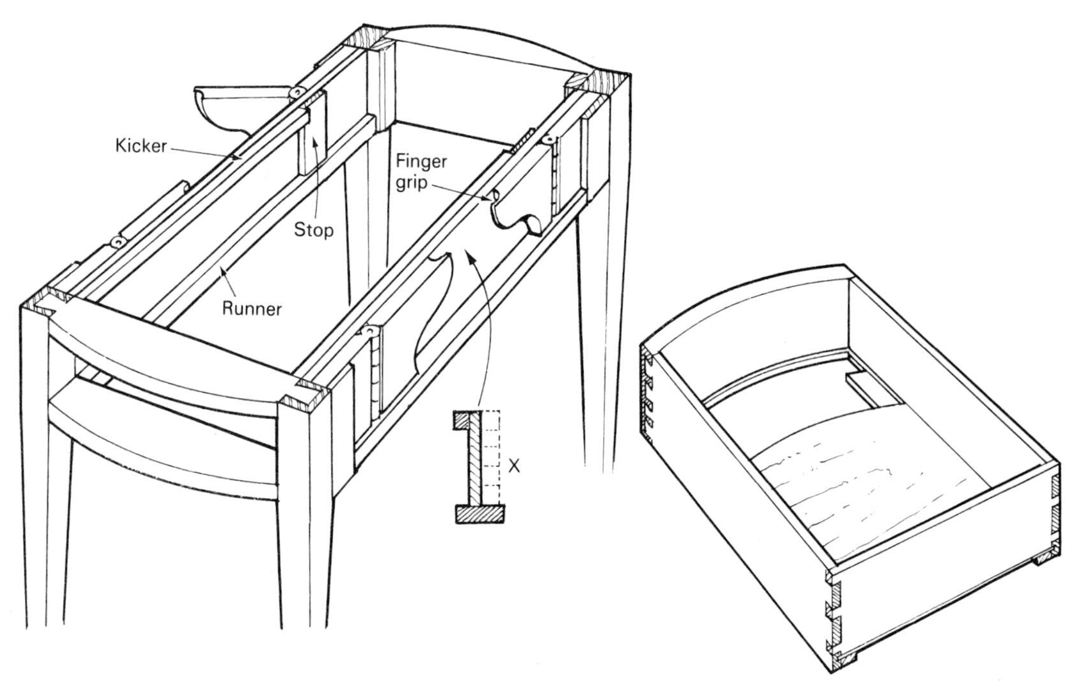

Fig. 3 View showing framework construction

Fig. 4 How the drawer is made

the inside as shown in Fig. 3, and stops are fixed at the rear. The drawer is 19in. deep only.

It will be realised that when the flaps are down, part of the side rails is exposed, owing to the elliptical shape of the top; consequently small veneered pieces about $\frac{3}{16}$in. thick are planted on immediately against the legs, as in Figs. 2 and 3.

Drawer construction is shown in Fig. 4. Solid stuff is used for the bow front and, following invariable trade procedure, the inner corners are planed off square, in alignment with each other, so that the dovetails can have square shoulders. A groove is cut to receive the bottom, but at the sides, the bottom fits into rebates, with slips planted on beneath to support the bottom and to increase the bearing surfaces.

Knuckle joints are used for the hinged brackets, as in Fig. 3, the fixed pieces being glued to the rails as well as tenoned to the legs. Note the hollow finger-grips cut at the top. The neat rule joints between the main top and the flaps have unusually deep squares, compared with the rounded member (A, Fig. 2). This hingeing would have to be done before the elliptical shape was cut, though no doubt final trimming would follow later.

We may pause here to consider the method followed by the craftsman in the veneering. Clearly the edge would be veneered first, as otherwise it would be liable to be dragged off in use. Then he would probably have separated the parts, and put down the main veneers on all three, leaving a margin at the edge of about $2\frac{1}{4}$in. to allow for the cross-banding. Before the glue had completely hardened he would probably have set a gauge to the full cross-banding width of $2\frac{1}{2}$in. and run this around the edge, enabling the waste strip to be lifted away easily. No doubt the three parts would then have been separated again. The inner narrow banding would have followed, and as it was only $\frac{3}{16}$in. wide, it could be bent to shape and held in position with fine pins knocked partly in at the outer edge. The main cross-banding would have been pieced with joints at fairly close intervals, especially at the more acute parts of the curve. A similar process would have followed at the outer banding, which is in the region of $\frac{1}{2}$in. wide. The narrow inner inlay lines could be bent round, and the cross-banding fitted up to them in pieces. Finally the outer lines would be fitted.

Another possible method, after putting down the main veneers on the separate parts, would have been to trim the veneer at the rule joints, and re-hinge. Battens would then have been screwed to the underside to keep the whole rigid, and the entire cross-banding then done around the elliptical shape as a whole, the advantage of this method being that the gauge could be used right across the rule joints. On completion of the cross-banding and inlay strings, a straight-edge could have been cramped along each joint in turn and a cut made right through the veneer with a keen chisel, or possibly a fine-toothed saw, enabling the parts to be separated.

French-Hepplewhite chair, late 18th century

Of all chairs made in the eighteenth century this must have been one of the most challenging to the chair-maker. There is not a straight line in it, and nearly all the curves are in fact compound. It is probable that when the first one was put in hand, a mock-up dummy was made beforehand, and shavings taken off here and there or pieces planted on, to correct any distortion in shape. The fact is that it is impossible to make a preliminary drawing which will show exactly the shape every part has to be. Compound curvature is a tricky business. A shape which appears pleasing when viewed from one direction may look distorted and ugly when seen from another, and there must have been considerable trial and error before a satisfactory and elegant chair was produced. The craft of traditional chair-making was essential because allowance had to be made, not only for any carving, but because of the fact that the various surfaces constantly changed direction, so that, say, a moulded detail might have to be resolved from one surface into an adjoining one. In addition, there were the complicated joints which had to be essentially strong yet unobtrusive. Of course the chair-maker, having produced the first, could repeat the design time and time again, templates of the various shapes being kept for future use.

Fig. 1 Mahogany chair, late eighteenth century

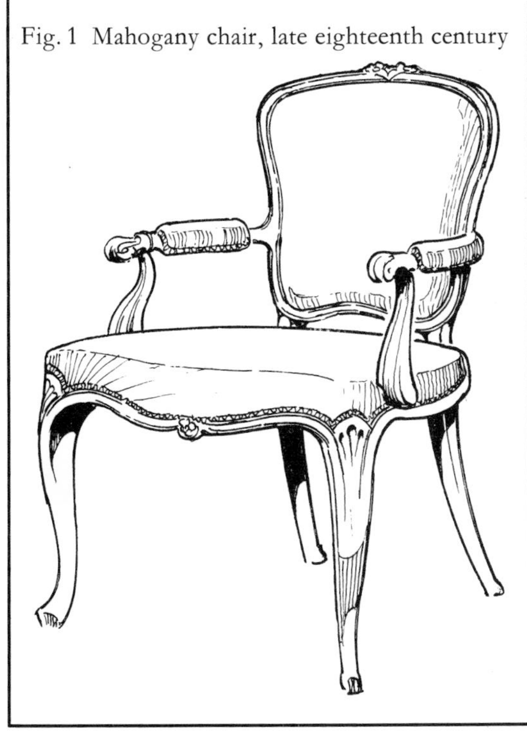

Any man attempting to make the chair in Fig. 1 would be well advised to make a dummy in softwood, omitting carved and moulded detail (although allowing for it). He would have to start with a full-size drawing, plans and elevations, realising, however, that some of the shapes could not be plotted in purely front or side elevation. The purpose of the drawing would be that of a general guide, and would have to be revised when the work was actually put in hand. As an example, the back legs are set to align with the curve of the seat, and are therefore at an angle somewhere in the region of 43 degrees. It is therefore necessary to set out this angle in the plan and erect elevations as at C, Fig. 2, and put in the curves on the adjacent faces. That is the way the craftsman has to work. He decides on the minimum section of timber required and wins his shapes from it. The reason is partly one of economics, but it is also because too great a width in timber might involve loss of strength across the grain. It might also cause distortion owing to shrinkage. The total of these considerations is that restrictions in width and thickness result in a dignified shape, free from overdone curvature. It is yet another example of how practical considerations have affected design. This applies specially to the parts in question, the back legs, which necessarily have to be strong to take the weight imposed upon them, yet they require a section of no more than 4in. by $2\frac{1}{4}$in.

The chair-maker (as distinct from the cabinet-maker) would have realised, from his experience with other chairs, the necessity for leaving extra thickness, not only for carving or other detail, but also for any edges which might have to be chamfered at an angle, owing to the semi-circular plan shape of the seat. Even so, his first experience in making such a chair must have caused him furiously to think – hence the preliminary mock-up.

Fig. 2 Scale drawing of the chair. **A** front elevation; **B** side elevation; **C** rectangular section from which back leg is cut; **D** true shape of back leg; **E** plan of seat; **F** seat framing showing leg positions and webbing

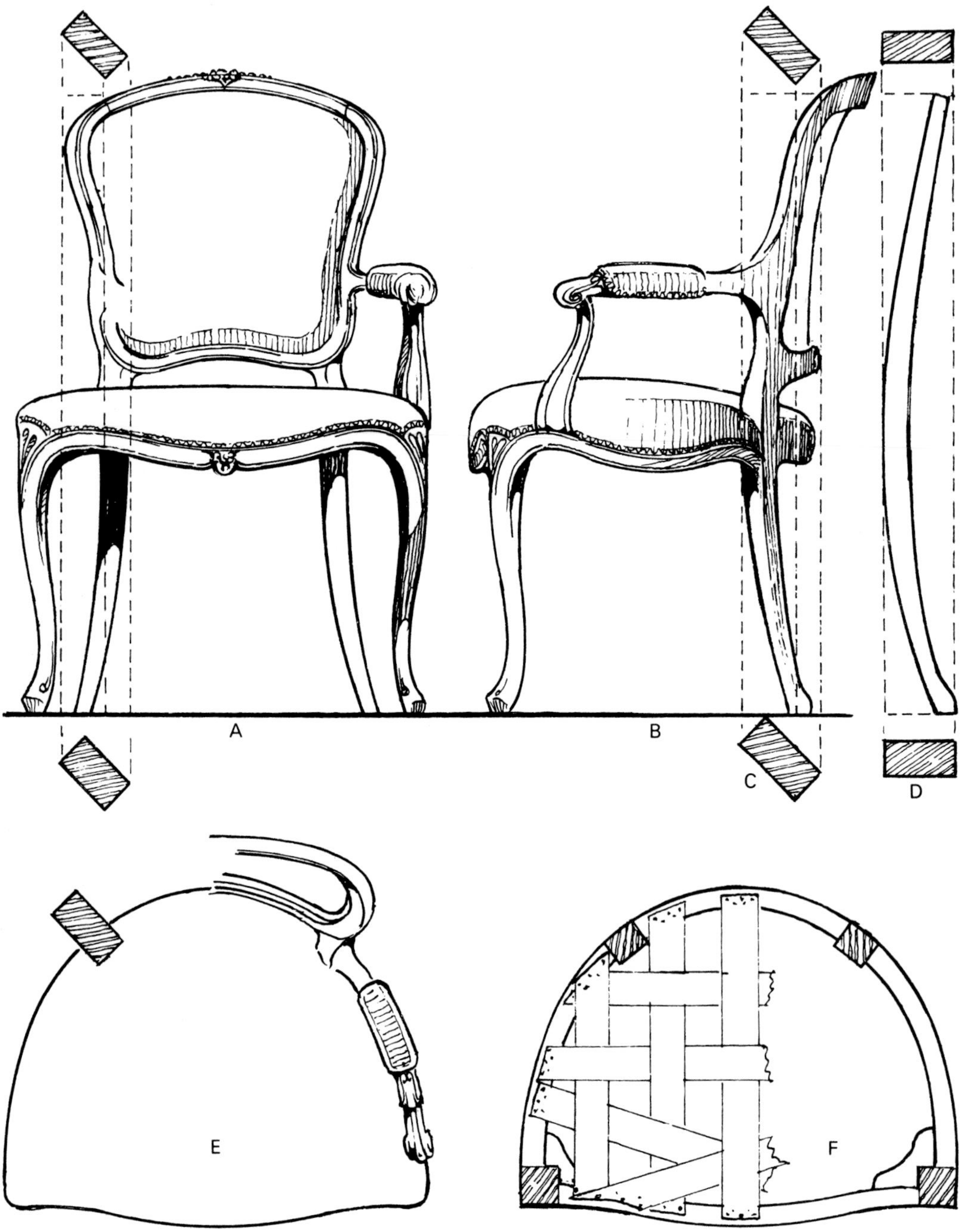

The front legs would not have presented any great problems because they are set square with the front, though they have to be designed so that the serpentine moulded band flows into them in an unbroken sweep, remembering that the front rail curves in plan as well as in elevation. The same applies to the side rails.

A rather different problem arises in the back legs, which are contained between the back and side seat rails, owing to the plan shape of the seat, F. In other words, the mortises for the rails occur on opposite sides of the legs, not on adjacent sides. The width of 4in. is needed because of the rake of the back, and a thickness of 2¼in. is necessary to enable the wavy line of the back, including the rebate into which the upholstery is tacked, to be cut as shown in Fig. 4.

Fig. 3 shows how the seat rails are tenoned into the legs. They are mostly about 3in. deep at the widest, and it must have called for some accurate sawing in such thick wood. No doubt the betty-saw was used. Cleaning up at the ends would enable the tenons to be marked out and sawn, leaving the shaping at the lower edge to be cut later.

The top and mid back rails have vertical shoulders where they join the back uprights, though those at the top appear to slope because

Fig. 3 Exploded view showing construction
Fig. 4 How back legs are plotted in rectangular sections, 4in. by 2¼in.

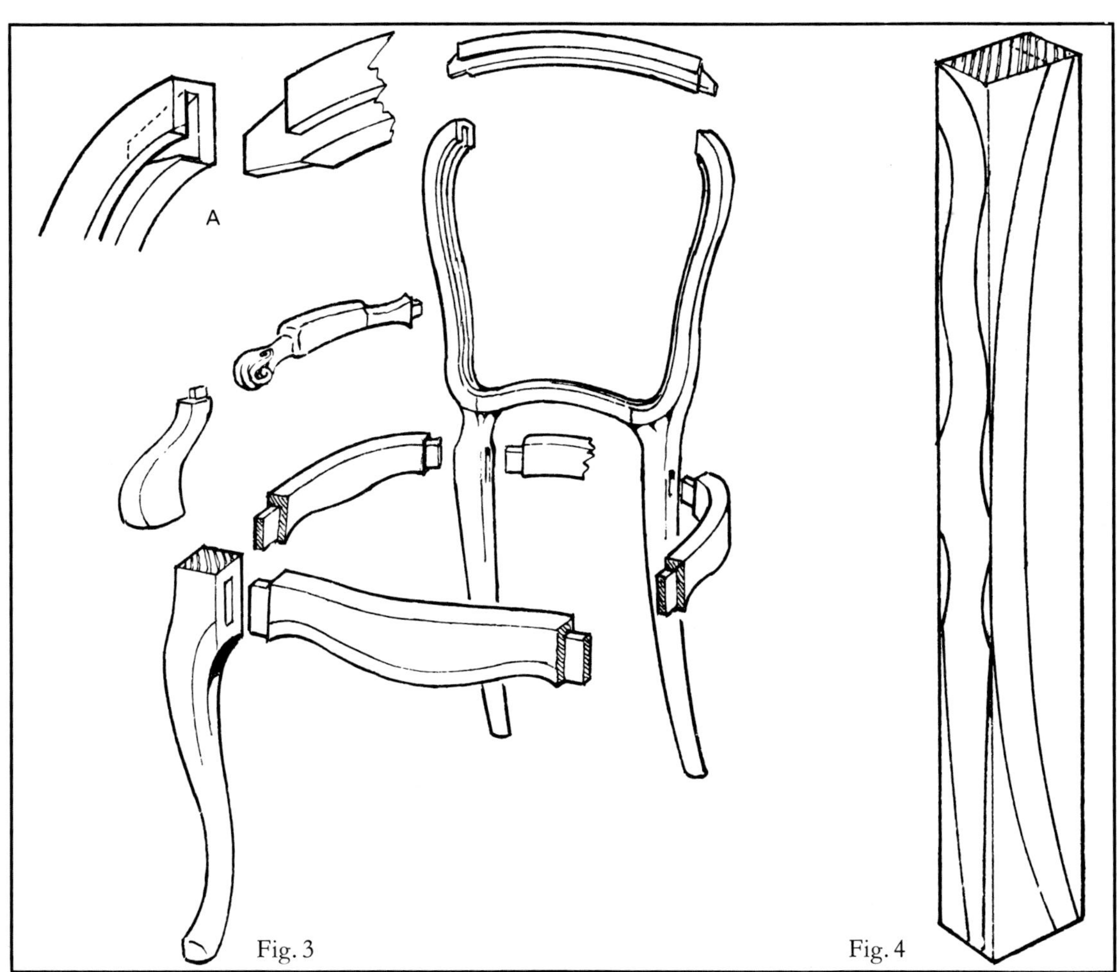

of their rounded section and the curved shape of the back. An awkward joint is involved, as shown in enlarged detail at A, Fig. 3. Here the whole thing is shown square in section, and the probability is that the craftsman did the entire jointing before working the rebate and finishing the shaping. Note that the top of the tenon has to slope so that it has maximum length and width without its mortise emerging at the outer edge. Final trimming would be done after assembly so that the whole had fine sweeping curves in both elevation and plan.

Much of the moulding of the back and seat rails could be done with the scratch-stock, though at parts the carver would have to take over. All chair-makers had a special form of scraper in which the cutter was set vertically, its great advantage being that it could be used on the varying direction of the grain without tearing out. A man might have a dozen or so of these scrapers with varying shapes of cutters. Of course they could only be used for preliminary cleaning-up before the moulded bands could be formed with the scratch-stock.

Kidney-shaped lyre table, late 18th century

Drawn from the original in the possession of Messrs Restall, Brown & Clennell, Cosgrove Hall, Milton Keynes.

Although the lyre was a popular motif towards the end of the eighteenth century and into the following one, it is extremely rare to find it in a table in combination with a plan of kidney shape. Doubts have indeed been expressed as to whether this table is entirely in its original form, though it is undoubtedly of old construction in detail. The whole thing is in satinwood veneered on to hardwood, except for the top itself which is veneered on softwood.

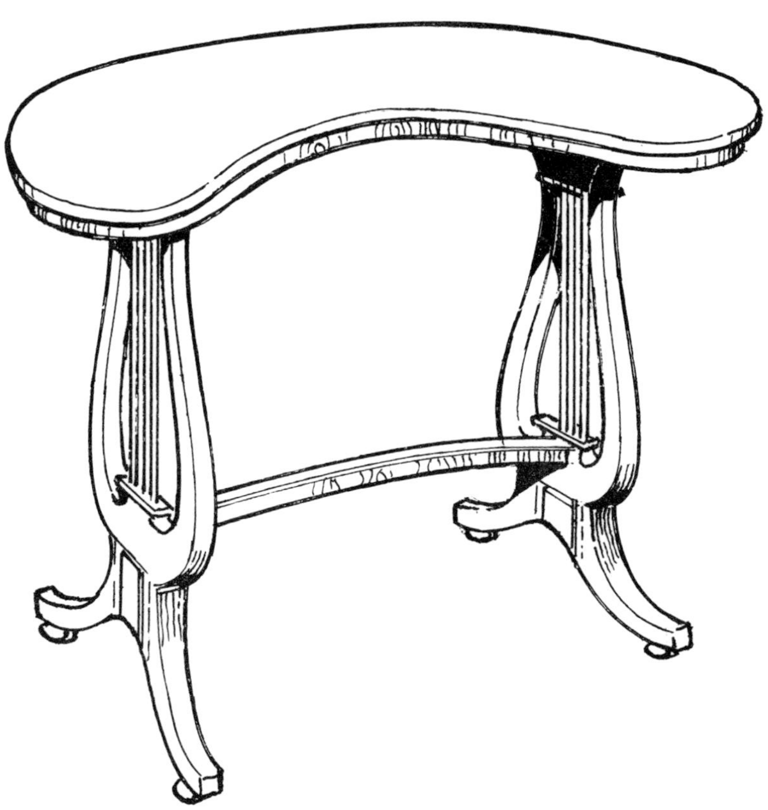

Fig. 1 Lyre table with kidney-shaped top

Shaped work invariably involves some awkward problems of construction, and no doubt the maker had his crop of difficulties to overcome. There was first the kidney shape of the top itself which needed a stiffening rim beneath, and a sound means of fixing it to the lyre framework beneath. Although it is possible to set out a kidney shape entirely geometrically, it is never really successful as it has a disjointed appearance. The much better way is to draw it out freehand, and this was done in the present case, as is obvious from Fig. 2. To the left is the main outline of the top, and to the right the edging which runs parallel with it all round. This edging is 1⅜in. deep and, since it is veneered on the outside, must have been assembled as a unit before the top was added, as otherwise it would have been impossible to level the joints, let alone lay the veneer and clean it up afterwards.

The usual way of making the edging would have been to make up the shape by the 'brick' method in two or possibly three thicknesses with staggered vertical joints, but this does not appear to have been done in the present case as there are eight shapes of single thickness, apparently put together with halved joints. To this edging are added two rails running from

Fig. 2 Plan with top partly removed and front and side elevations

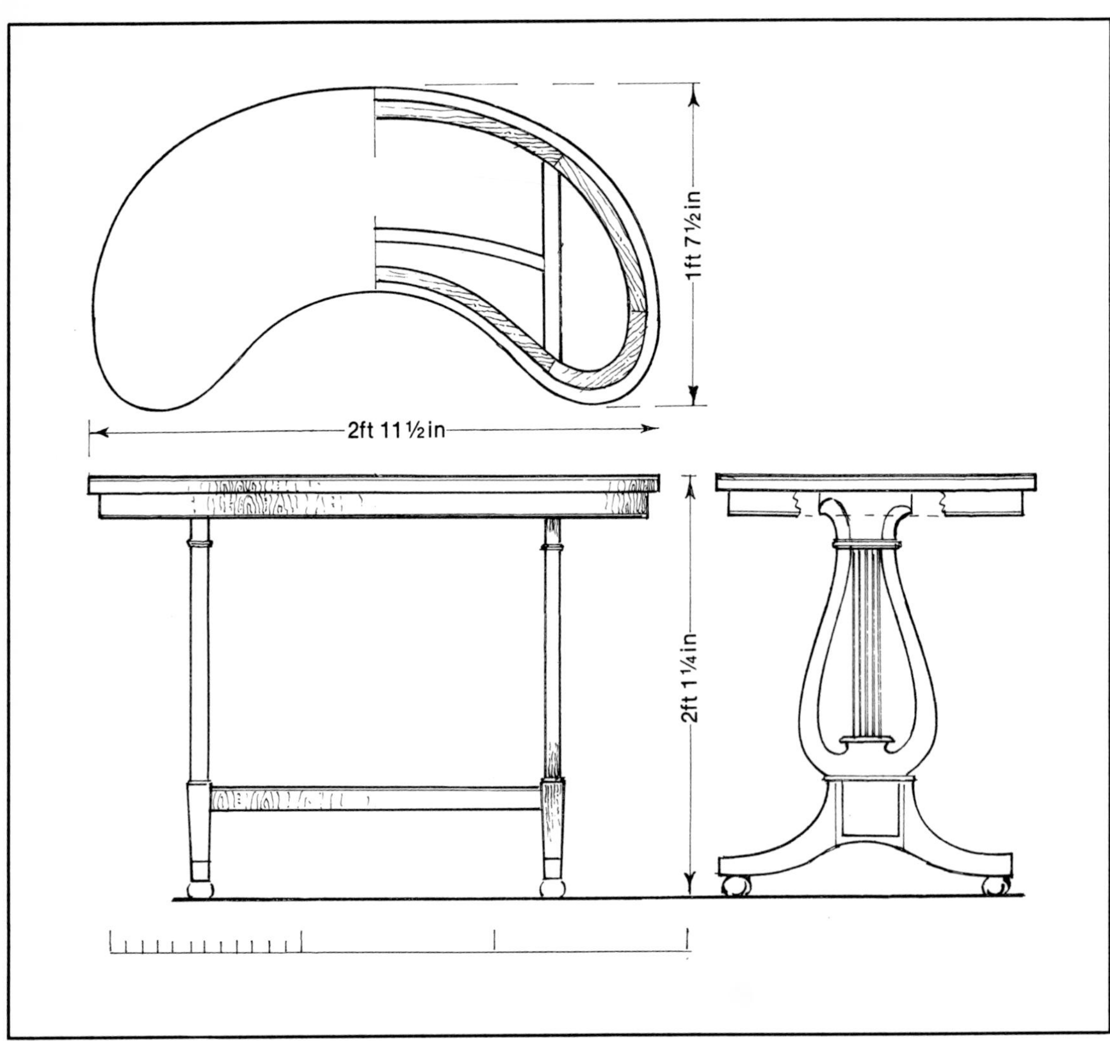

front to back to form a fixing for the lyre ends. Screws were used to fix the top itself to the edging, and around the top and beneath the edging is a dark inlay line.

Construction of the lyre ends is given in Fig. 3, and it will be seen that many pieces were used to form the shape. At the top, the main curved uprights are tenoned into a piece the grain of which is horizontal, and the shape is continued into this. A narrow astragal moulding conceals the joint. At the bottom the curved uprights are tenoned into a block, again with horizontal grain direction, and into this piece are fixed the shaped legs with slot-dovetail joints. Metal rods are used to form the 'strings', and these, of course, would be fitted before the top member was added. A small decorative panel is fixed to the outer side of the cross piece into which the legs are jointed.

Finally there is the curved stretcher rail joining the two lyre ends. It is veneered with cross-grain at sides and top, with inlay lines at the edges. Mortise and tenon joints are used to join it to the lyre ends.

Fig. 3 Construction of lyre ends

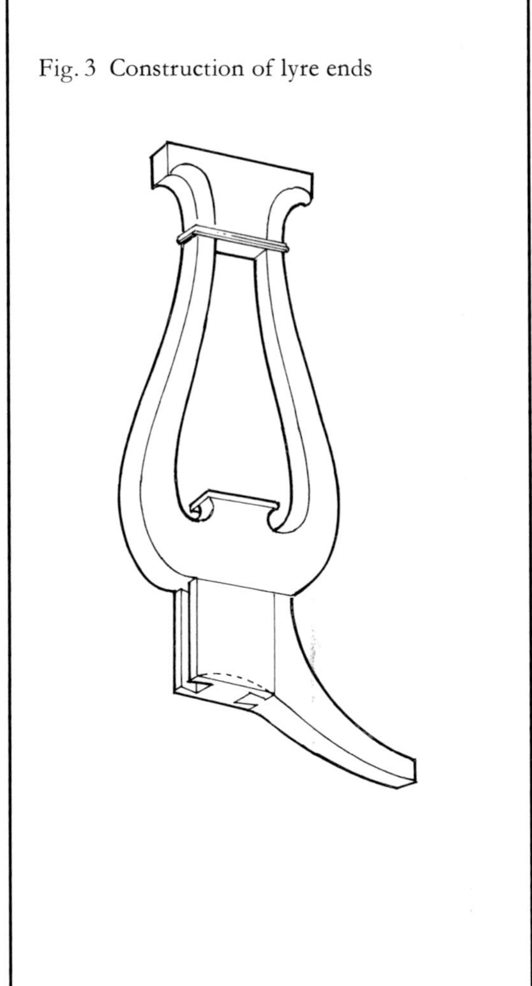

Mahogany chair of the late 18th century

Fig. 1 Mahogany chair

This type of chair was fairly common from about 1780 onwards, and is generally associated with the Hepplewhite school, though Hepplewhite's *The Cabinet Maker and Upholsterer's Guide*, 1794 edition, does not include a chair with this type of back. The pattern was not so expensive to make as, say, the shield back, of which many are included in the book, but it certainly called for the skill of an experienced chair-maker. No doubt any firm specialising in chair-making kept sets of templates of shapes so that repeat orders could be turned out without difficulty. Any piece of work involving compound shaping called for experience because the alteration of a curve in one plane could easily give a distorted appearance when viewed from a different direction. This is particularly true of chair work, but once a shape appeared satisfactory it could be used for all similar models in the future.

It is interesting to see how practical considerations entered into the design of chairs. An apparently involved compound shape was often produced from a relatively small section of timber. For instance in the present chair the back uprights were cut from timber no more than 3½in. wide by 1⅞in. thick. This is shown by the dotted lines in Fig. 2. By setting the upright at an angle in the front elevation, the curvature is more apparent than real. The same applies to the top shaped back rail. The shape of this is largely dictated by the fact that it is joined to the uprights with mortise and tenon joints, and the curves are so planned that the tenons can have maximum length without danger of the mortises being exposed at the outside. Even so, the outer edge of the tenon has to slope to avoid the curve. A shape of greater lateral slope would curtail the tenon so severely as to be impracticable. It is a good example of how a characteristic yet attractive shape has been evolved out of practical necessity. In any chair involving compound shaping, the first thing to find is the square section of timber needed for the shape. The greater the section needed, the more expensive it is to make (and incidentally the greater the risk of distortion, unless in experienced hands).

Fig. 2 Scale elevation and seat plan. **A** front elevation (back sections at **X** and **Y**); **B** side elevation; **C** seat level plan; **D** arm plan shape; **E** side seat rail showing how tenons wind; **F** side seat rail front tenon; **G** side seat rail back tenon

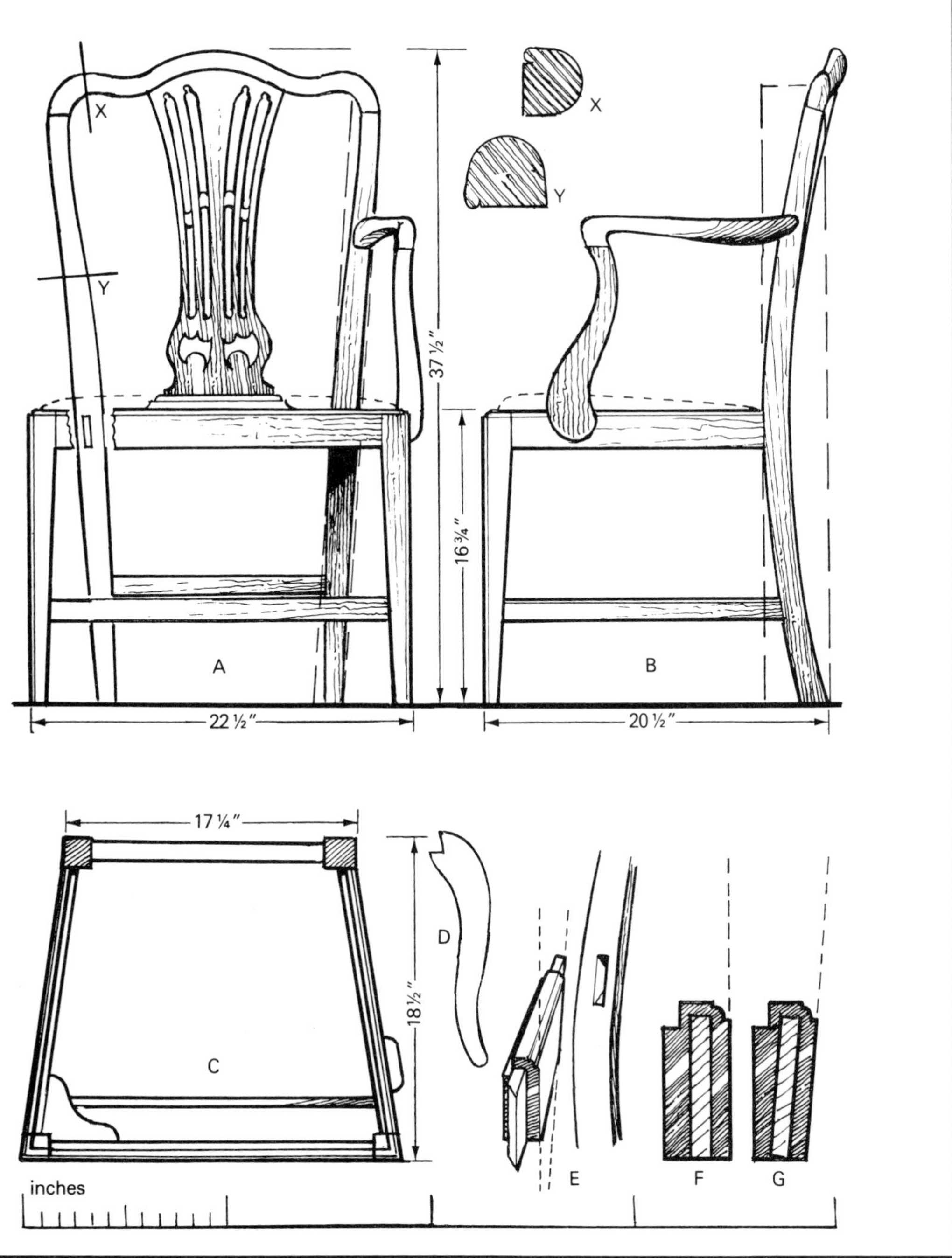

General construction follows the usual lines, all the joints being variations of the mortise and tenon. There are however one or two points calling for consideration. One which is often not realised by the inexperienced man is that the front and back tenons of the side seat rails are not in the same plane, but wind, one with the other. This is because the back legs converge towards the floor whereas the front legs are vertical. Thus the back tenons have to slope at the same angle as the back legs, as shown at E, F, and G, Fig. 2. In practice the chair-maker, after making the rails straight and square, would plane the outer surface towards the back at the same angle as the slope of the back legs, thus enabling him to use the mortise-gauge from the outside to mark the back tenons. The dotted lines at F and G, Fig. 2 make this clear.

Since the mortises in the legs have to be at an angle aligning with the plan shape of the seat, some form of guide for holding the chisel was necessary and the usual chair-maker's dodge was to cramp the leg over a tapered block of

Fig. 3 Parts separated showing joints
Fig. 4 Loose seat frame
Fig. 5 Tapered block used when mortising legs

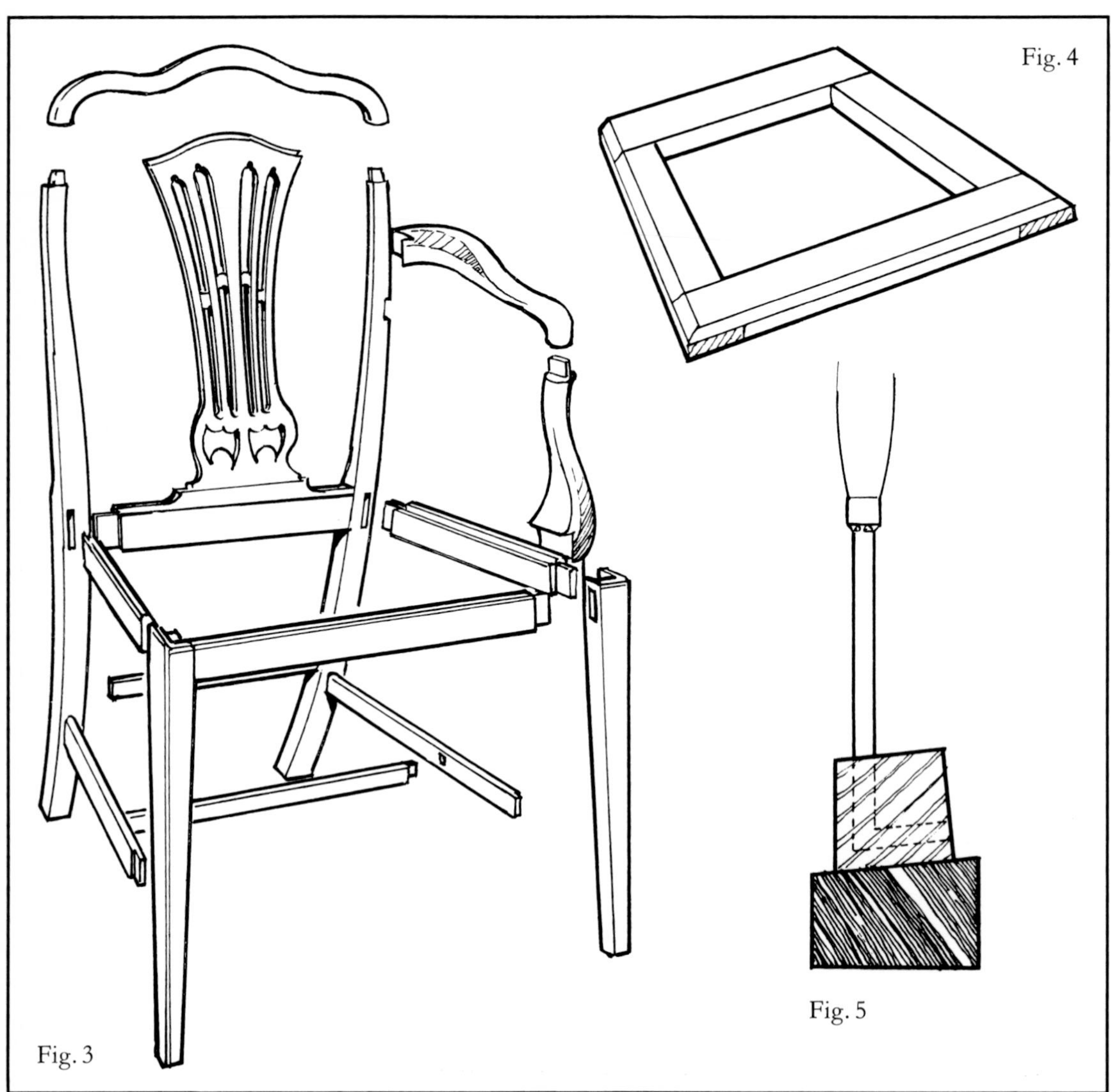

wood, the slope of which agreed with the plan angle, as in Fig. 5. In this way he had only to hold the chisel upright to ensure a cut at the right angle.

In a chair with a loose seat-frame it was usual to rebate the side and front seat rails, partly to provide support for the seat-frame, but also to reduce the visible thickness of the rails at the top. To avoid reducing the rails unnecessarily the rebate depth has been kept at only $\frac{1}{2}$in. although the seat-frame is $\frac{7}{8}$in. thick. By working a chamfer around the edges as in Fig. 4, the upholstery does not rise in an abrupt curve at the edges but slopes gradually away. In common with many old chairs the loose seat-frame in the present chair is a replacement. Successive recoverings of the seat invariably result in innumerable tack holes, with the consequence that the wood splits badly. In making the frame, a gap of $\frac{1}{8}$in. is allowed all round for the thickness of the covering material, and all sharp corners are taken off so that they do not cut the material. Incidentally, the upholsterer's method of doing this was to give each corner a clout with the hammer. The frame might be put together with either halved, or mortise and tenon joints.

Since the top back rail is slightly dished, a thickness of $2\frac{3}{4}$in. is necessary, although the rail finishes only $1\frac{3}{8}$in. at the ends and 1in. at the middle. It also has to be at least an extra inch long, as in Fig. 6, so that when the mortises are chopped at the ends there is no danger of the wood splitting. Although the inner end of each mortise is square, the outer end slopes slightly so that there is no danger of its becoming exposed when the shape is cut. Dishing the wood in plan would be the first operation, and since this would necessarily remove any marking of the front elevation shape, a template of the shape would have to be bent to the hollow for marking out.

Fig. 2 shows that the back uprights and top rail are rounded at the back, and have a small bead worked at the outer corner, as at X and Y. Much of the rounding would be done before assembling, but final levelling would be needed at the joints. Another essential operation would be to cut the groove to receive the top of the splat. To do this a form of router with a fence at one side (the old-woman's-tooth variety) would be needed. It would need a stout cutter of groove-width, and would be used like a scratch-stock. It would be done after the lower shape of the rail had been cut and trimmed, but before the top shape was sawn. In Fig. 7 the splat is omitted to reveal the groove to receive it. This illustration also shows how the small bead is worked with the scratch-stock. This would be done after assembling the entire back.

Incidentally this splat, although finishing $\frac{7}{16}$in., requires a thickness of $\frac{7}{8}$in. as it follows approximately the backward curve of the uprights. At top and bottom it has to be barefaced tongued to fit the top rail and the shoe (the raised piece fixed to the top of the back seat rail). In cutting the openings, holes would be bored at the top and bottom to enable the saw to be passed through. Those at the top would be the actual small circular holes used in the design.

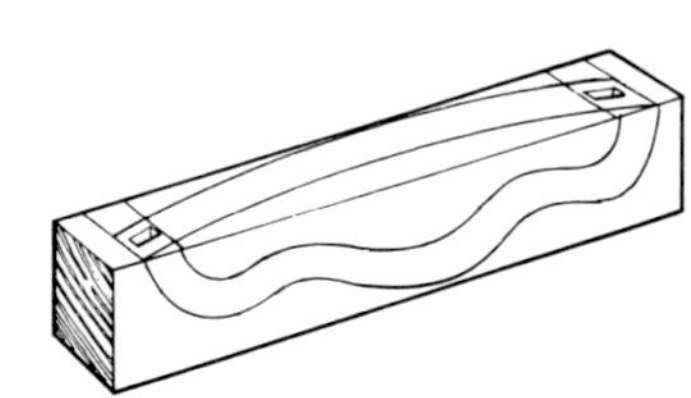

Fig. 6 Top back rail marked out and mortised

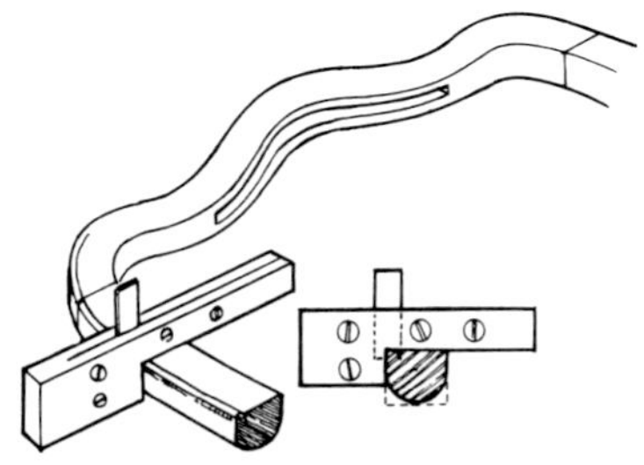

Fig. 7 Bead worked with scratch stock around back

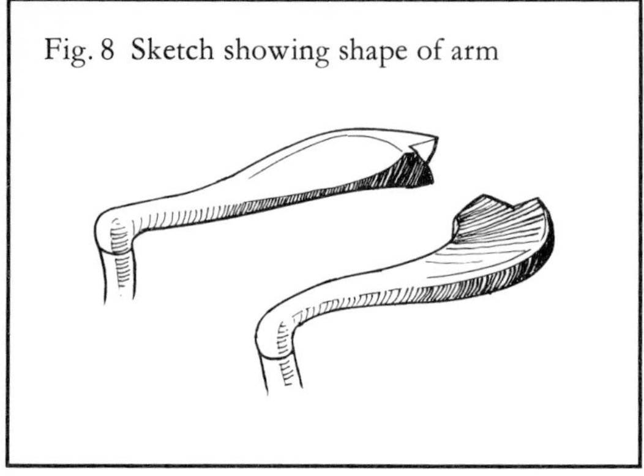
Fig. 8 Sketch showing shape of arm

There is something characteristic about the shape of the arms and their supports. At the top the arm is practically flat, though sloping inwards slightly, but as it reaches the front it resolves into a nearly circular section, Fig. 8. At the juncture with the back it is cut to fit into a notch and is held with a counter-bored screw driven through the upright, the hole being pelleted afterwards. At seat level, the support is cut away locally in the form of a shallow halving, and is held with screws driven through the rails. A mortise and tenon is used to join the arm to the support; clearly the mortise would have to be chopped before the shape is cut, otherwise the wood would split.

The rebate and small ovolo moulding worked around the seat-rails are of course worked before assembly, but both have to be continued into the legs, and this is more conveniently done after the whole has been glued up.

Mahogany bookcase-cabinet, last quarter of the 18th century

Fig. 1 Mahogany bookcase-cabinet

Drawn from the original in the possession of Collins Antiques Ltd, Wheathampstead.

At first glance this cabinet appears to be a typical late eighteenth-century secretaire and bookcase, but the interesting feature about it is that the doors of the lower carcase reach right to the top, the drawer fronts being dummies. For some reason the entire lower carcase was required for cupboard accommodation. It was almost certainly not done for economy because, although the cost of fitting two drawers would be somewhat more, the saving would not be great compared with the cost of such a quality cabinet as a whole. In fact the costly work of veneering, inlaying, and cross-banding would have been the same whether drawers were fitted or not.

If such a piece were made today the doors would be of good grade multi-ply or laminboard because these materials are free from shrinkage. Obviously this was impossible at the period when this cabinet was made, and the cabinet-maker used a board of solid wood for each door, veneering the face to resemble drawer fronts and separate doors. He mounted the whole thing on a framework of mahogany as shown in Fig. 4. As it happens the choice of method was unfortunate because the doors have warped badly subsequently, not merely in width, but also in length. It has since required drastic treatment to correct the trouble. Of course, the use of curl mahogany veneers for the ovals made things difficult, especially as such veneers were sawn by hand and were quite thick. The probability is that the veneers proved stronger than the groundwork and took charge of things, pulling the latter and the framework out of shape.

Main construction of the piece is shown in Fig. 3. Lapped dovetails are used for the lower carcase. The ends reach right to the floor, and, to enable the French curved feet to be cut, blocks are glued on at the outside as shown. After levelling, the whole was veneered. Lapped-dovetails were also used for the book-case portion, and the ends were trenched to

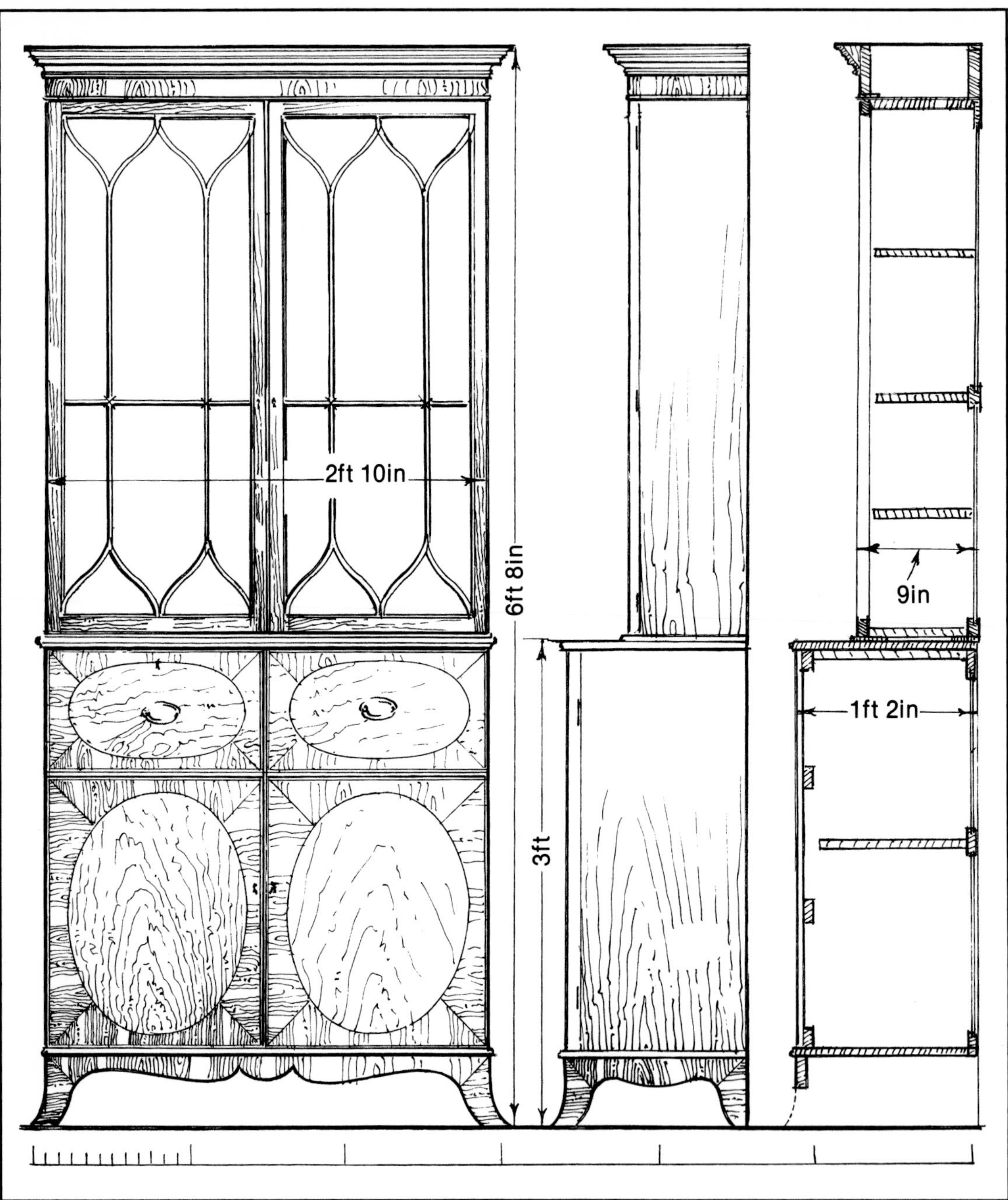

Fig. 2 Scale front and side elevations and side section

enable shelf heights to be adjusted to suit the books.

An attractive feature of the bookcase doors is the double-ogee tracery, the section being a $\frac{3}{8}$in. astragal mounted on $\frac{1}{8}$in. rear bars. No doubt the craftsman followed the usual practice of fitting a softwood panel into the rebate of the door and marking out the design on this. He then fitted the various mouldings on to this, glueing just the mitres so that the whole held together. The panel was then removed, the

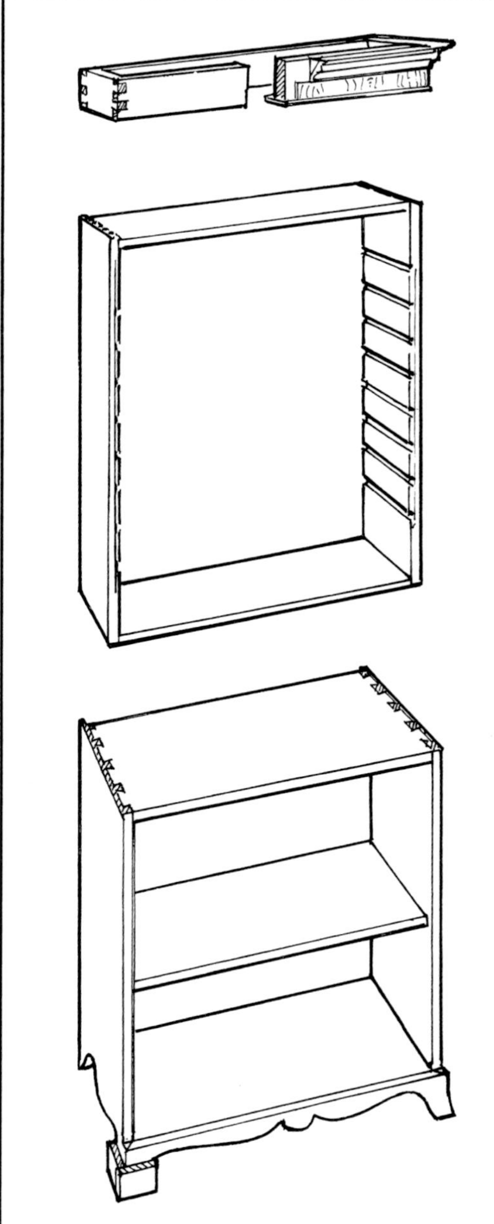

Fig. 3 Construction details showing cornice, upper carcase and lower carcase

door turned face down, and the stiffening bars glued on at the back, the ends fitting into notches in the framework.

Incidentally some craftsmen prefer to work the other way round, fitting the rebate bars first then adding the mouldings. All told, however,

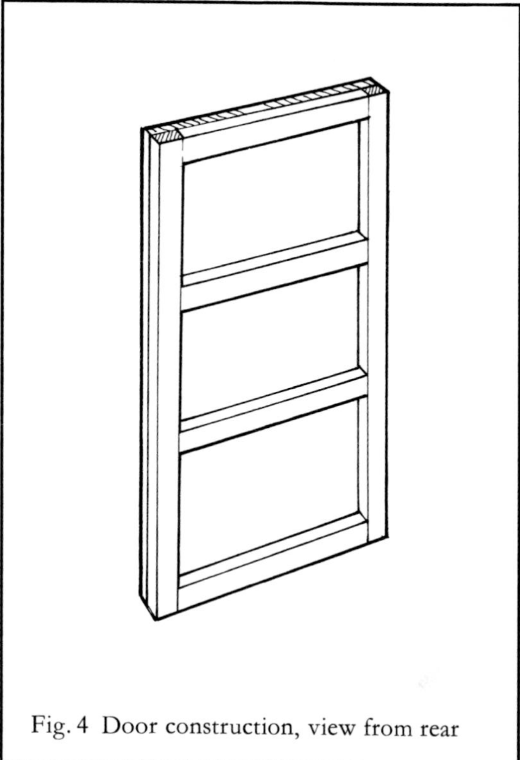

Fig. 4 Door construction, view from rear

the former method makes for greater accuracy as the mouldings are the more important, and the parts are assembled on the marked out panel itself. When set and after polishing the glazing is put in with a form of coloured putty.

A separate cornice is fitted as shown in Fig. 3, consisting of a dovetailed framework cross-veneered on the lower part and with cornice moulding planted on above. Such cornices were usually loose and were held in position by corner blocks fixed to the top of the carcase beneath.

Sheraton period chair, about 1795

Taken generally, Sheraton chairs were rather simpler than those immediately preceding them, the reason being that compound curvature was mostly avoided. Compare Fig. 1 for instance with the French-Hepplewhite chair on page 64. In the latter there is scarcely a straight line anywhere, and nearly every curve is shaped in both plan and elevation. On the other hand, in this Sheraton chair the only double curvature is in the top back rail which is bowed in plan and curved upwards in elevation. The chair in Fig. 2 provides an interesting comparison; it, too, has little or no compound curvature.

Fig. 1 Sheraton period chairs, about 1795

Fig. 2

Fig. 3 Scale drawing of chair. **A** front elevation; **B** side elevation; **C** plan of top back rail; **D** back and leg sections; **E** plan of seat rails

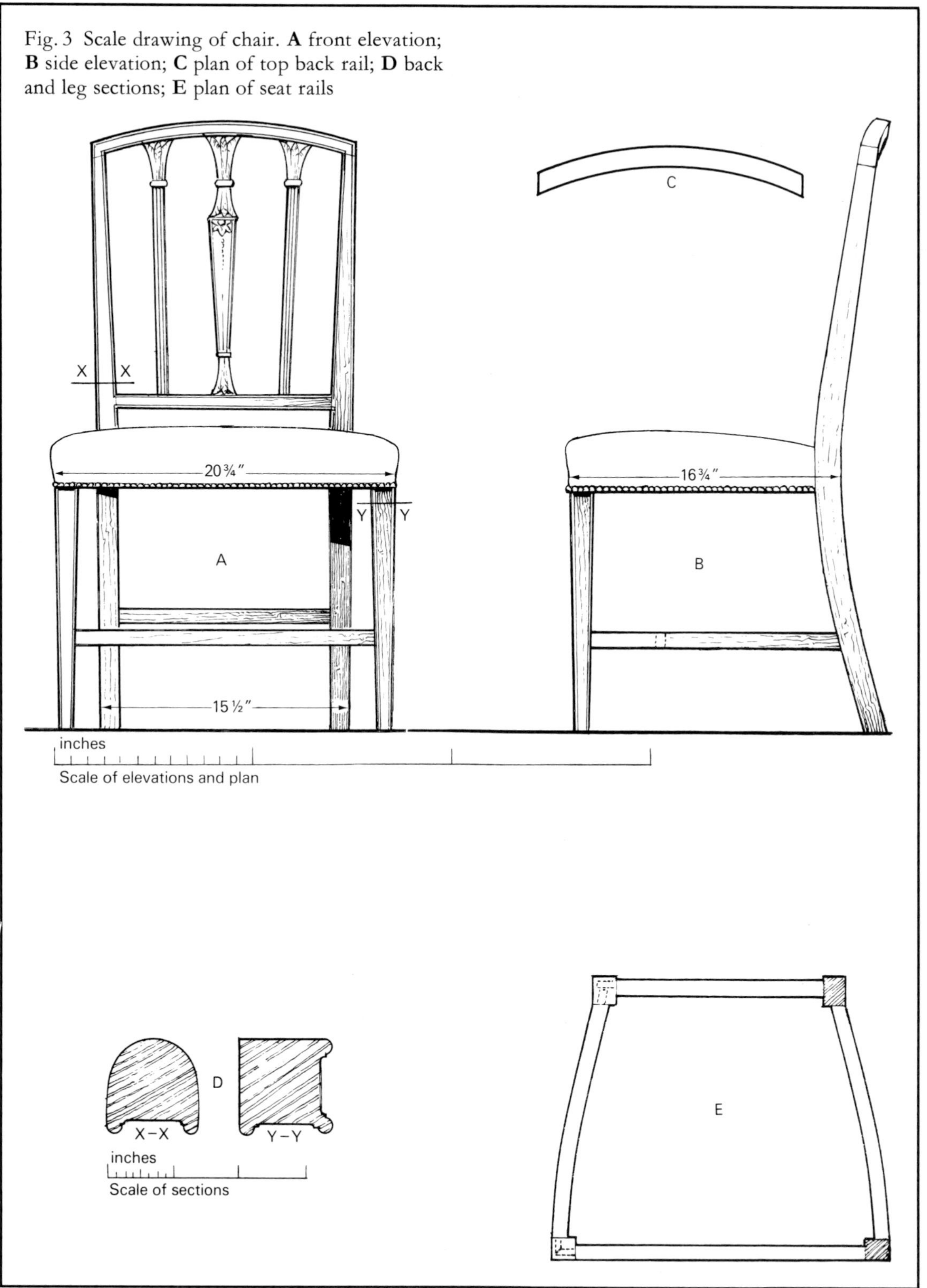

At the same time it should be realised that, although simpler in this respect, both chairs in Figs. 1 and 2 would call for a high degree of skill in the making. For such light chairs to be really strong, the best workmanship would be needed. The first-class chair-making work and skilled carving are a remarkable combination. In Fig. 2 it is difficult to see where the carver had to take over from the bench-hand. For instance, the moulding of the back members would be done by the chair-hand, using the scratch-stock, first from one edge then from the other, but where the mouldings appear to pass one over the other, or to meet at a mitre worked in the solid, the carver would be needed.

In both chairs, the side seat rails are curved in plan, as shown at E, Fig. 3. The legs are square in section and the rails flow into them in a continuous sweep, enabling the upholstery also to be in an unbroken curve. At the rear it does not matter, because the covering ends at the back legs. This detail is true of most, though not all, stuff-over chairs. Those with caned seats might have either curved or straight side-rails.

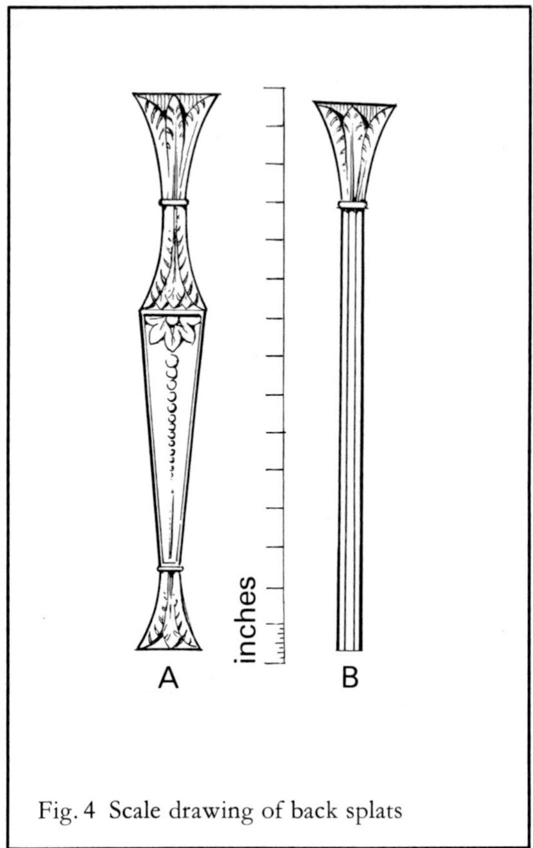

Fig. 4 Scale drawing of back splats

Mahogany secretaire about 1790

Drawn from the original in possession of Collins Antiques, Wheathampstead.

Although the secretaire was a quite common item in the eighteenth century, a feature that calls for special comment in the present example is the domed cornice. Today, and indeed at any time during the last hundred years or so, there would have been no special problem in that it could have been worked easily on the spindle-moulder. But how was it done when only hand methods were available? Obviously a moulding-plane could not have been used because the latter has a straight sole and can be used only on a straight surface. Clearly then the only way was to use the scratch-stock, with some of the preliminary work done with a specially-made rebate thumb plane to ease the task of using the scratch-stock which in its nature is necessarily laborious to use in that it merely scrapes rather than cuts the wood.

Probably the craftsman in realising this decided to make the moulding in two pieces as in Fig. 4, the lower hollow member and the upper ogee. Even so to use the scratch-stock only would have involved some really hard work, and I have suggested in Fig. 6 the stages in which the hollow member was probably done.

Mahogany was a costly imported wood, and ways of economising its use were common. Consequently most cornice mouldings were made with a facing of mahogany on which the actual members were worked and a backing of softwood. A straight cornice would be simple enough – in fact Sheraton in his *Cabinet-maker and Upholsterer's Drawing Book* gives detailed instructions on how it was done. In the present case however the matter is complicated by the domed shape. I have not much doubt but that the craftsman followed the method indicated in Fig. 6. A section through the moulding showing the facing and backing is given at (A), and (B) shows how the two curved pieces would have been glued together flat on the bench. The positions of the members were marked at the ends and gauged round the curve. This indicated the extent to which the edges had to be

Fig. 1 Mahogany secretaire with front closed

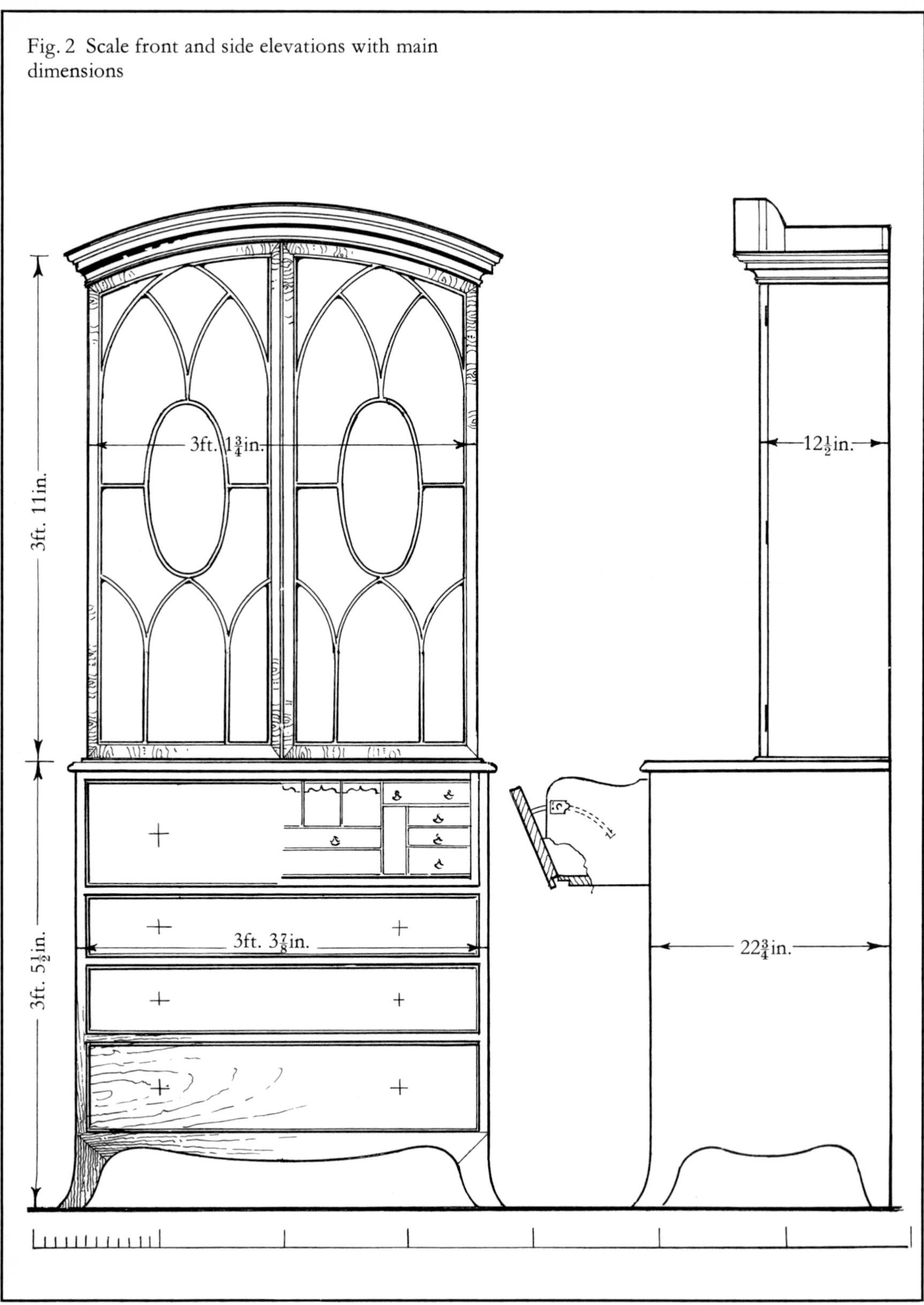

Fig. 2 Scale front and side elevations with main dimensions

Fig. 3 Exploded view showing construction

chamfered at right angles with each other; also the top and bottom squares again at right angles as at (C). This enabled the work to be placed with its back surface flat on the bench as at (D), and a series of rebates cut with a curved thumb rebate plane. It is quite likely that the craftsman used a gouge to reduce further the hollow to the required section before using the scratch-stock to finish off. I rather think he made up a special tool as in Fig. 7 with two bearing surfaces so that there was no risk of the tool tending to leave the edge and so digging in sideways, and there must have been the two rubbing surfaces marked X so that the tool ceased to cut when the full depth was reached. The smaller members would follow and the upper ogee made in the same way.

So much for the domed cornice itself but clearly the actual top of the carcase itself had also to be curved, and a pretty formidable task faced the craftsman since there was a rise of about 4½in. at the middle, this necessitating a piece of wood 5½in. thick. To reduce this to shape, the simplest way would have been to make a series of saw cuts across the grain and chop much of the waste away with the chisel before finishing with a form of compass plane. Quite likely he gave this laborious but unavoidable job to an apprentice.

Since this top had to be lap-dovetailed to the ends, flats would have to be left on the underside at the ends in alignment with each other so that they could bed down into square sockets cut in the ends as in Fig. 3. After assembling the projecting corners at the top would be trimmed level with the top, but since large glue blocks had to be added later the levelling would be flat to enable the glue blocks to be planed flat and bed down onto a flat surface. Otherwise their undersides would have to be slightly hollow.

As the front cornice had to stand immediately above and in front of the doors, an arched rail had to be fixed halfway down the thickness of the top (Fig. 4). This would have been a somewhat flimsy fixing, and to strengthen it a series of large glue blocks, actually touching each other, were rubbed in all round at the back angle, these being afterwards rounded over at the top as shown.

Clearly the return mouldings at the ends had to be of a different section from that at the front, because of the top curve and also because the width varies although the projection from the face remains the same. This is shown at X, Fig. 4.

To make the shelves variable in height, a series of grooves had to be ploughed across the ends. Every cabinet-making shop of any size must have possessed such a trenching tool. The grooves would have been worked before the rebate for the back so that any splitting out at the back edge was taken out in the subsequent rebating. On a quality piece like this the panelled back was justified, though many such pieces had the simpler muntin back.

Traceried doors with shapes were a rather tricky task, and it would be essential to fit a panel into the back rebate on which the design would be marked out to enable the various

Fig. 4 **A** section through cornice and doors, **X** is section through side returns; **B** drawer side showing dovetails; **C** section through drawer side; **D** brass handle

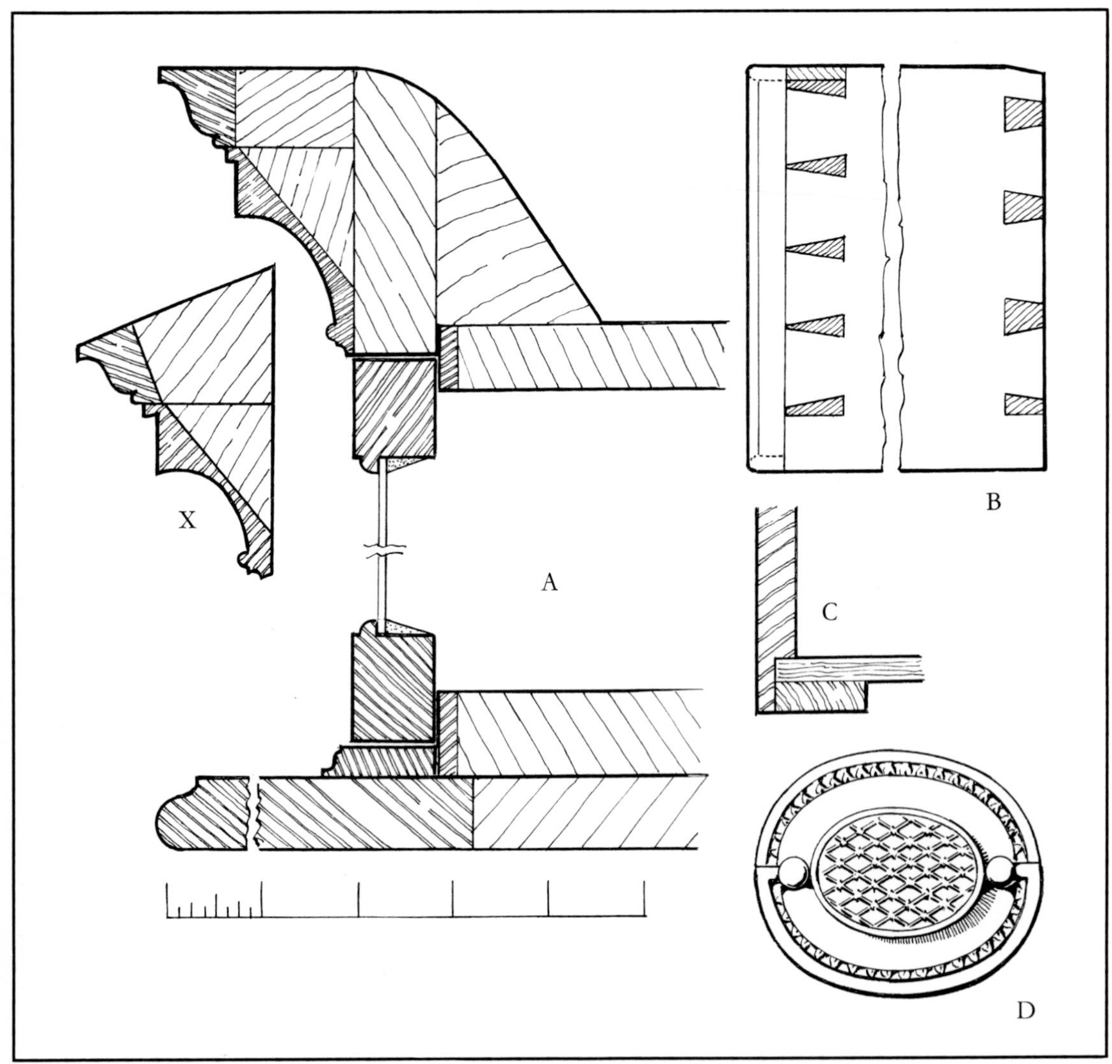

parts to be assembled. Probably the centre ellipses would have been made up first as a whole and placed in position, the other parts being added afterwards. Mitres would be cut at the intersections and would have been given a touch of glue to hold them.

To enable the back bars to be added the panel would be removed, the door reversed on the bench, and the panel placed beneath to give support. Frequently back rebate bars were cut in the solid, but a stronger method (mentioned by Sheraton) would have been to laminate them in three thicknesses of veneer bent around shaped formers. Where they join the main door framework they were let into small notches. Halving joints or small tenons were cut where the bars join each other.

Details of drawers are given in Fig. 4 at (B) and the bottom fitting at (C). Grain of the bottoms runs from side to side and in this piece are in mahogany throughout. Usually oak was used for all parts except the fronts. An attractive feature are the curved French feet. In construction the ends run right down to the floor, the front apron fitted into mitred ends, and blocks glued into shallow rebates at front and sides to enable the shape to be worked. Afterwards the whole was veneered.

Fig. 5 Secretaire open

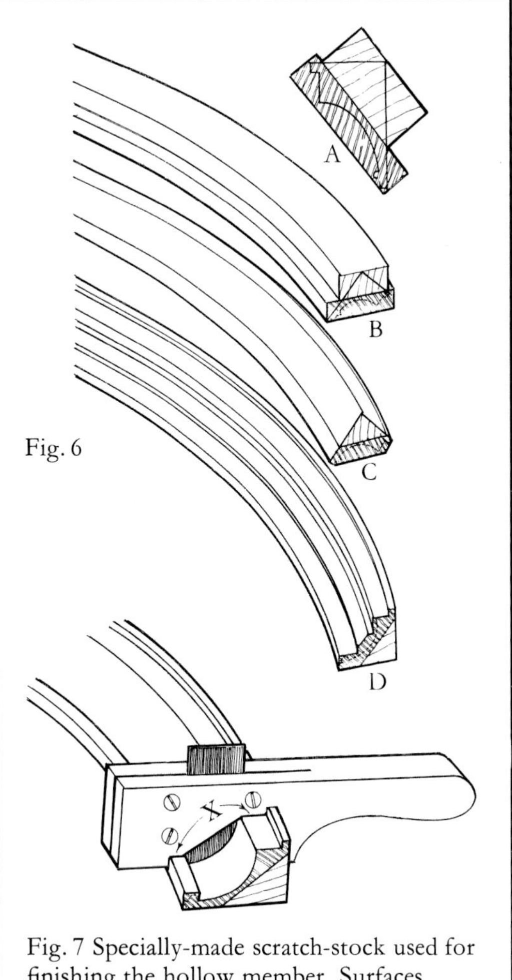

Fig. 6

Fig. 7 Specially-made scratch-stock used for finishing the hollow member. Surfaces marked **X** act as stops

Serpentine-front chest of drawers, about 1790

Drawn from the original in the possession of Collins Antiques Limited, Wheathampstead.

During the second half of the eighteenth century, and especially in the last quarter, large numbers of chest of drawers were made, all following a general pattern but with variations in shapes and detail. In its simplest form the chest had a straight front and might have four to six drawers or even more. Variations much sought-after today are bow- or serpentine-fronted, and Fig. 1 is an example of the latter. Such chests were necessarily expensive to make because, apart from cutting into a great deal of timber, they took considerably longer to make than the straight type. Drawer fronts were

Fig. 1 Mahogany serpentine-front chest of drawers

invariably veneered – they had to be because, apart from the cost of cutting in solid wood, it would not have been practicable to cut them by hand methods. In some cases the fronts were 9in. or 10in. deep and to saw the shape in such thickness would have been impossible. This was the problem facing the eighteenth-century cabinet-maker, and he solved it by using what can be conveniently called the 'brick' method.

Having set out the plan shape he cut a series of 'bricks' in softwood, usually $\frac{7}{8}$in. thick but sometimes thicker. Each 'brick' followed a part of the curve, and these were glued one above the other on the setting out. Strength in the length was ensured by staggering the vertical joints as shown in Fig. 5. The inner surfaces were then levelled and cleaned up. Fronts, too, were levelled approximately, but, before veneering, the entire drawers were jointed and assembled except for the bottoms, and fitted to the carcase. This enabled the craftsman to place the whole thing on its back on the floor, and complete the cleaning of the entire front. In this way all the drawer fronts and drawer rails were made perfectly level and in alignment over the entire front surface. Veneering followed and finally the cocked beads were added.

Fig. 2 Scale drawing of the chest. **A** front elevation; **B** side elevation; **C** plan in part section

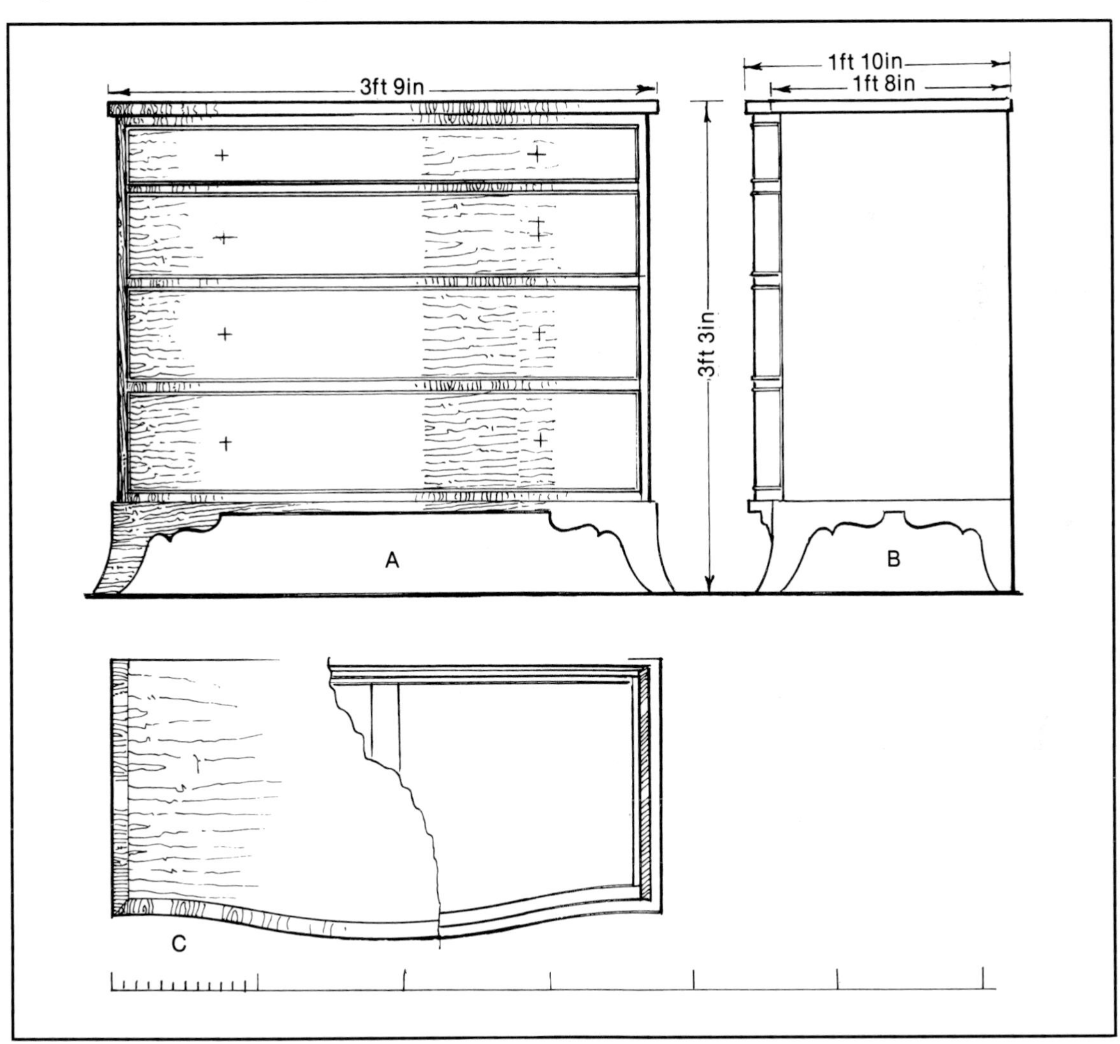

Construction of the chest in Fig. 1 follows the method more or less standard at the period. The bottom is lapped-dovetailed to the ends, and at the top are two rails with triangular brackets glued on to give stiffening support to the ends, Fig. 3. (Sometimes a solid false top was fitted, but the two rails with brackets were more economical of timber and enabled odd pieces to be used.) Drawer rails are stub-tenoned to the ends and the runners fit into and are supported by shallow grooves. Dustboards fit into grooves in the runners.

Fig. 3 Construction of the main carcase. **A** detail of French bracket foot
Fig. 4 (below) Stages in making the French bracket foot before veneering

An interesting feature are the French bracket feet, A, Fig. 3. They necessarily follow the plan curvature of the carcase but additionally they splay outwards at the bottom. Fig. 4 shows the

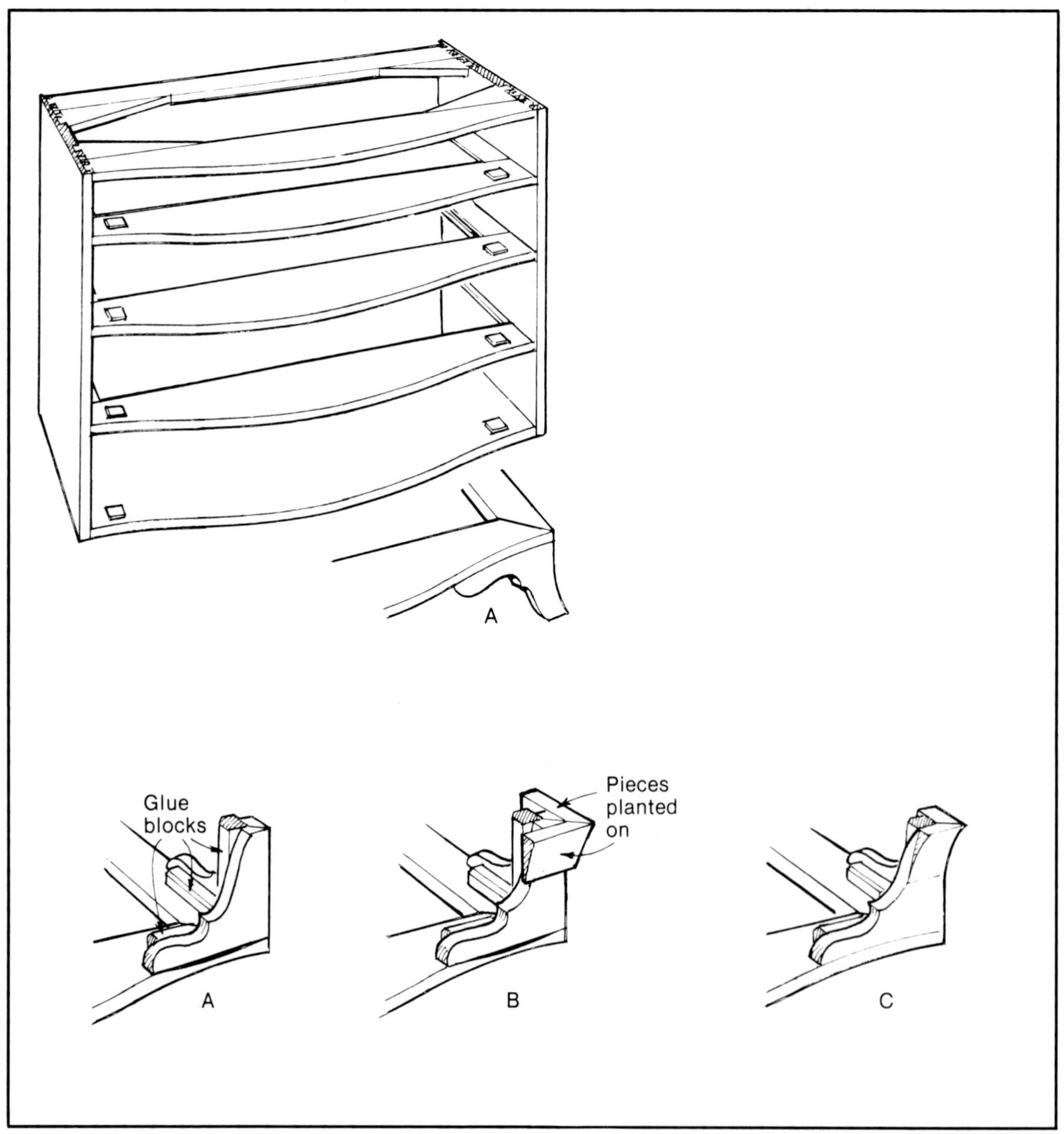

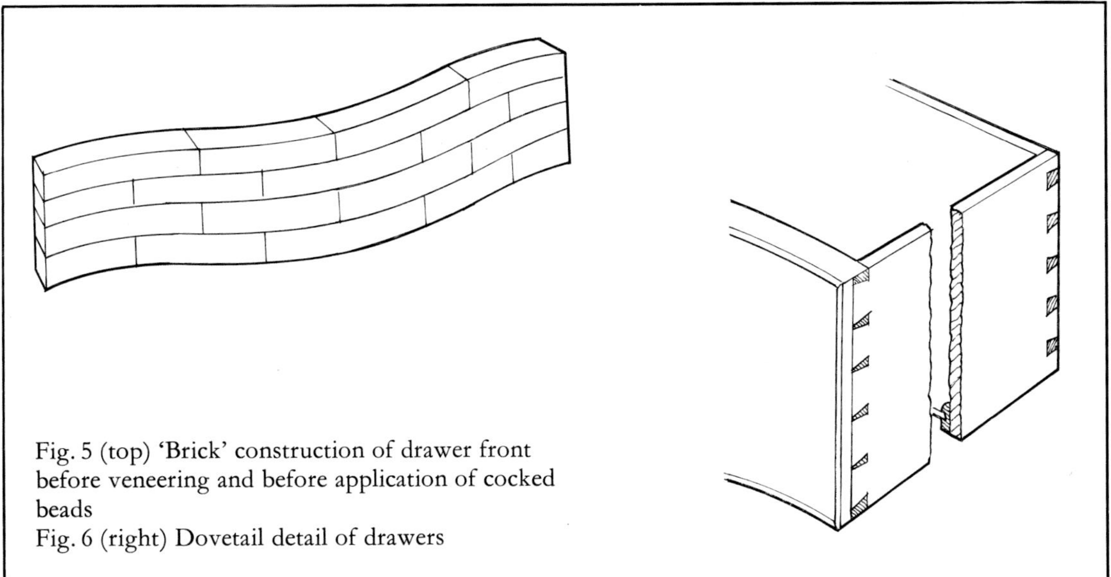

Fig. 5 (top) 'Brick' construction of drawer front before veneering and before application of cocked beads
Fig. 6 (right) Dovetail detail of drawers

stages in making such feet. In most cases the carcase ends would reach right down to floor level, the leg being built out. Here, however, there are flat rails beneath the carcase forming a framework, and the feet are fitted separately to this. The illustration shows how the work would be done, the framework lying upside-down on the bench. First the front and side would be cut to shape, fitted to the framework, and strengthened with glue-blocks as at A, Fig. 4. At this stage no attempt at plan shaping would be made. Two tapered pieces would then be planted on, and the corner mitred as at B. These two planted-on pieces enabled the outward splay to be worked as at C. Finally the plan shaping would be completed, the surfaces veneered, and lastly the shape of the foot would be sawn.

Bow-front sideboard, about 1800

Drawn from the original in the possession of Restall, Brown & Clennell, Milton Keynes.

Many bow- and serpentine-front sideboards of the late eighteenth and early nineteenth centuries were quite massive items made for the large rooms of their period, but occasionally one finds a small piece which is ideal for present-day rooms. That in Fig. 1 is an example, measuring only 40in. in length. If one were making such a sideboard today, no doubt square tapered legs with spade feet would be substituted for the turned type, as at D, Fig. 2, as they belong an earlier period and are more popular today. Curvature of the front in plan is relatively slight, there being only $1\frac{3}{4}$in. difference between the depth at the ends and at the middle. This makes for economy in that the drawer fronts etc. cut into only a minimum of wood.

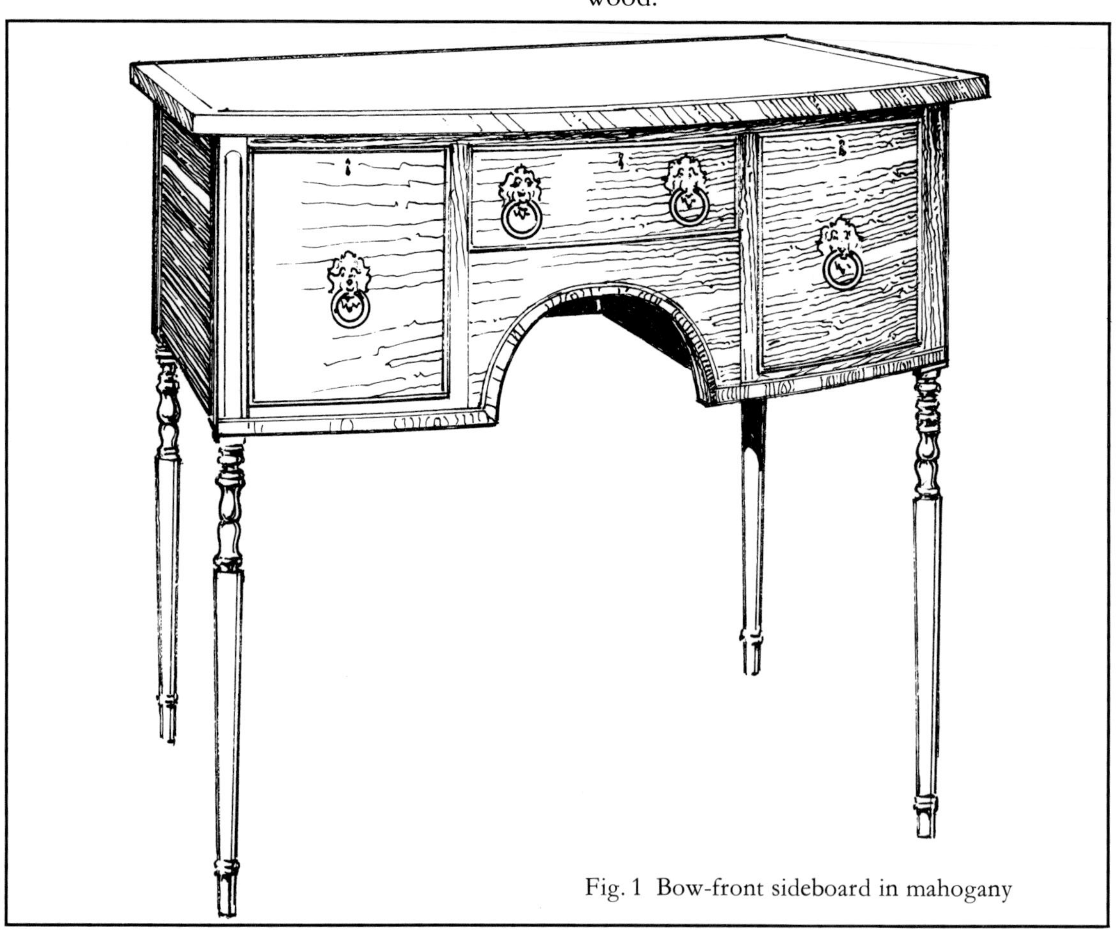

Fig. 1 Bow-front sideboard in mahogany

Construction at the period followed a general pattern, though it varied in detail. In most cases the back was a solid piece of $\frac{7}{8}$in. softwood tenoned into the back legs. At front was a top rail dovetailed into the front legs and end rails, with intermediate uprights through-tenoned and wedged into it (Fig. 3). Between these uprights is a centre drawer rail, and at the bottom are two drawer rails dovetailed to the uprights and tenoned into the legs. Anyone making a reproduction of the sideboard would take the sizes of these drawer rails directly from the main top rail which, of course, runs across the whole length.

In most cases each pair of front and back legs was joined by two end rails flush with the inside and with outer panels tongued into the legs. Behind the intermediate uprights are solid panels reaching to just above the centre drawer rails. Beneath the centre drawer rail the arched filling or apron consists of three pieces mitred and tongued together worked to shape and veneered. The whole is a push fit held with glue and glue blocks as in Fig. 4.

Drawer fronts are of pine veneered with mahogany and with oak sides and back. Bottoms are of pine with grain running from side to side. Cocked beads are fitted all round the fronts, that at the top occupying the full thickness. At sides and bottom the dovetails are reduced in length to enable narrow beads to be fitted in a rebate, Fig. 5. As the curvature of the drawers is quite slight, the cabinet-maker has not bothered to shape the inside of the

Fig. 2 Scale drawings of sideboard. **A** front elevation; **B** plan in part sections; **C** side elevations; **D** alternative tapered leg with spade foot

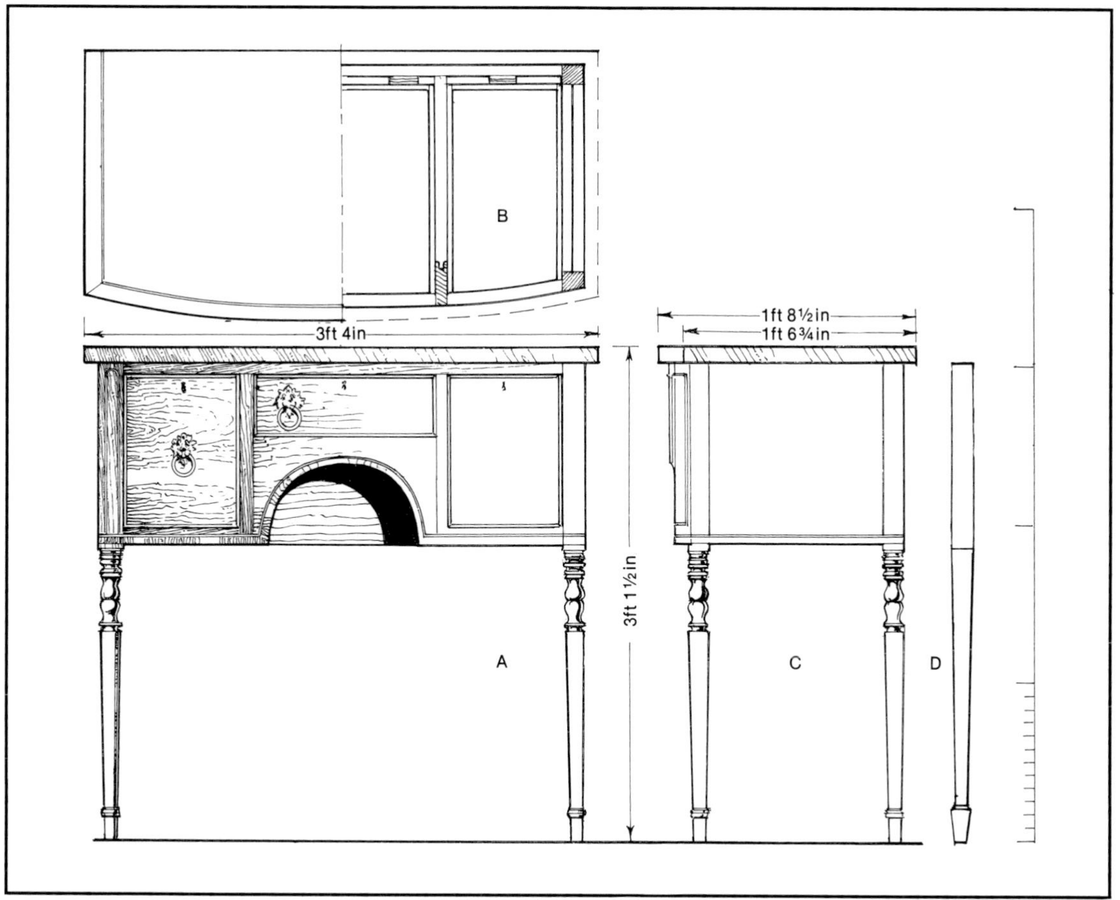

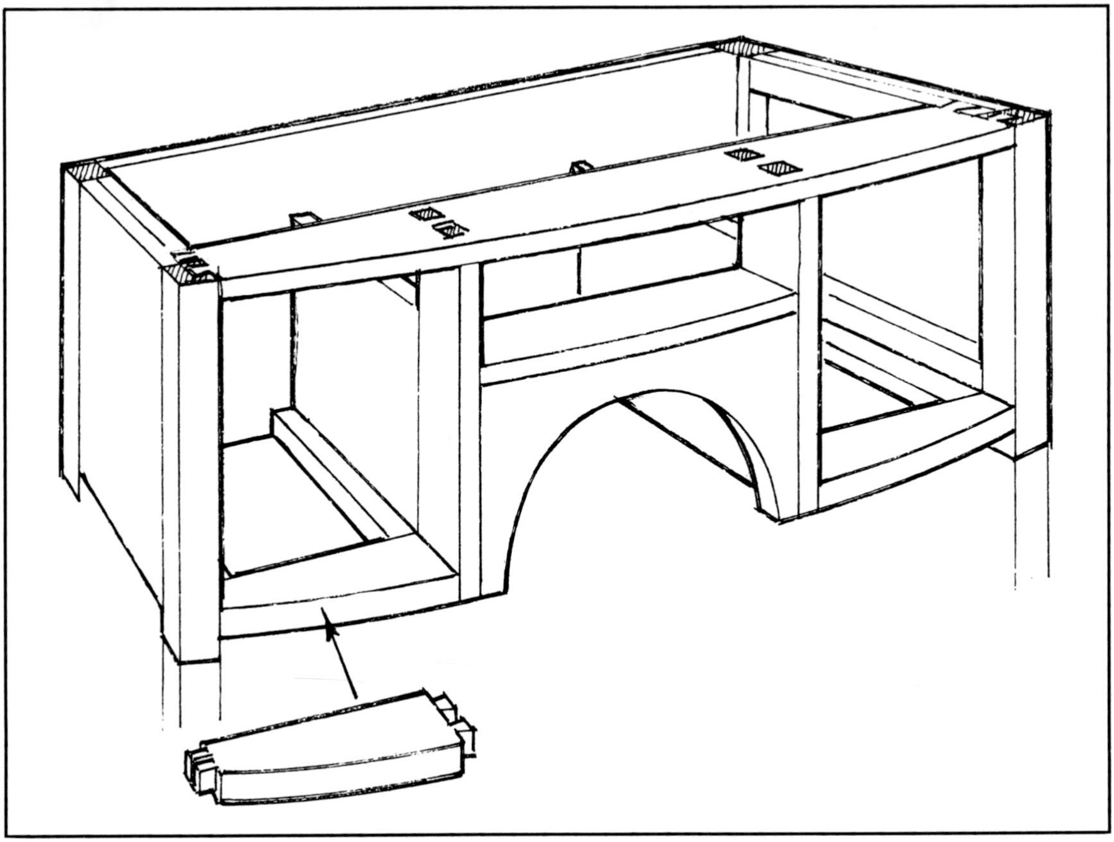

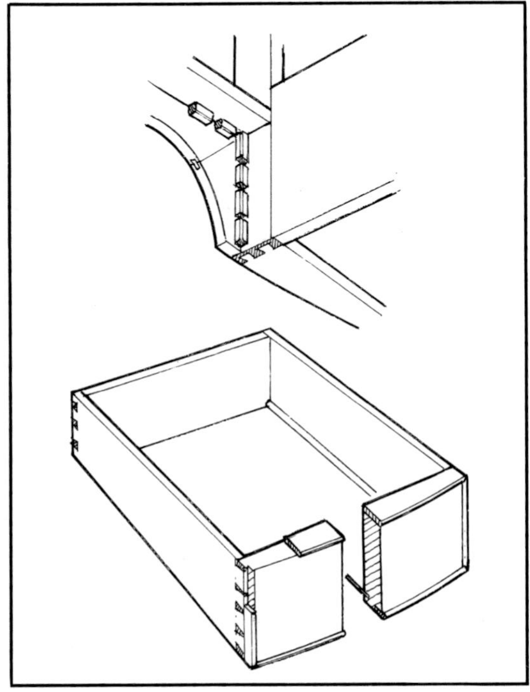

Fig. 3 Construction of sideboard
Fig. 4 (top left) View of apron from inside and beneath
Fig. 5 (below left) Drawer construction

fronts. It saved him an hour or so of work in hollowing out the inside.

An unusual feature is that the veneer around the edge of the top is at an angle rather than taken across square. The surface of the top itself has a cross-banding around the edges with an inlaid line, as shown to the left in Fig. 2, B. There is also a dark inlay line with cross-banding around the arched centre and continued beneath the drawers. Note too that the square upper part of the legs has an inlaid line finishing at the top in a semicircle. To cut the groove for this, the cabinet-maker no doubt made a template in thin hardwood or metal and worked a narrow chisel or similar tool around it with a scraping action.

Drawer construction

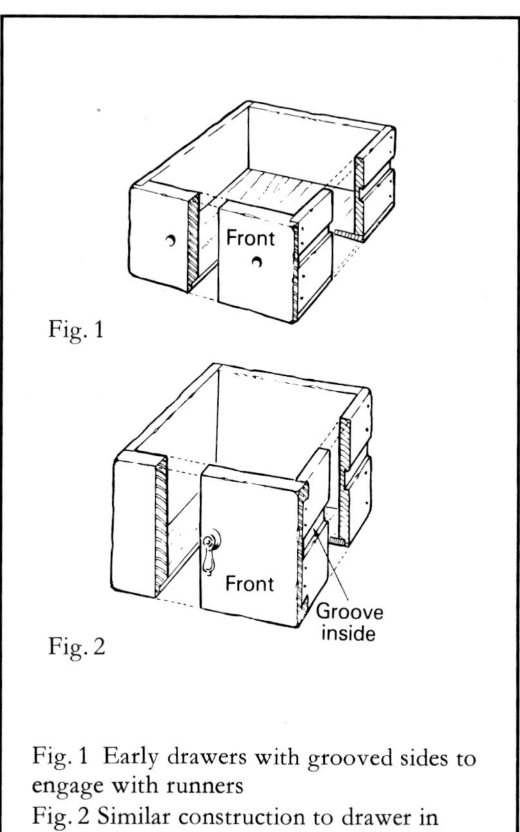

Fig. 1 Early drawers with grooved sides to engage with runners
Fig. 2 Similar construction to drawer in Fig. 1 but with single large dovetail at the front

Although it is possible in a general way to trace a sequence in the development of drawer construction, it is unwise to be dogmatic in dating a piece purely by the way the drawers were made. Quite often an older method was continued after new ways had been introduced, possibly because a craftsman was conservative enough to remain true to the method of his boyhood apprenticeship; or it may be that he was not equipped to adopt new ways. In some cases, it might be that the maker had to adapt his method to suit the size of timber available to him. Another possibility is that the maker was of continental origin and used the method familiar to him in his country of origin.

During the oak period, drawers were frequently made with grooves in the sides which engaged with runners fixed to the cabinet framework as in Fig. 1. To enable this to be done, the sides had to be fairly thick ($\frac{1}{2}$in. or more). Frequently the sides were merely fitted into rebates in the front and then nailed, and butted and nailed at the back. Alternatively there might be a single, rather coarse dovetail at the front, as in Fig. 2. The bottom might be fitted into rebates in the front and sides, or, more frequently, simply nailed beneath the sides and back, although the front might be rebated to receive it. Occasionally one comes across a drawer with rather coarse dovetails, as in the drawer shown on page 17.

It was not until the walnut period that drawer construction approached anything like standardisation, and even then early walnut period drawers were frequently quite crude, judged by later standards, and were unsatisfactory in many ways. For instance, rather coarse through-dovetails were often used to join the sides to the front, and the latter was then veneered. No doubt the underlying idea was that since the veneer covered the ends of the dovetails it did not matter. Such drawers may have looked satisfactory when first completed, but time and wear have taken their toll. In the first place, glue does not hold well over end grain, and the ends of the dovetails necessarily show end grain. Then, the slightest racking of the drawer resulted in movement at the joints and this caused cracking in the veneer. Admittedly early veneer was thick, as it was cut with the saw, but even so a certain deterioration was inevitable (as any experienced repairer knows).

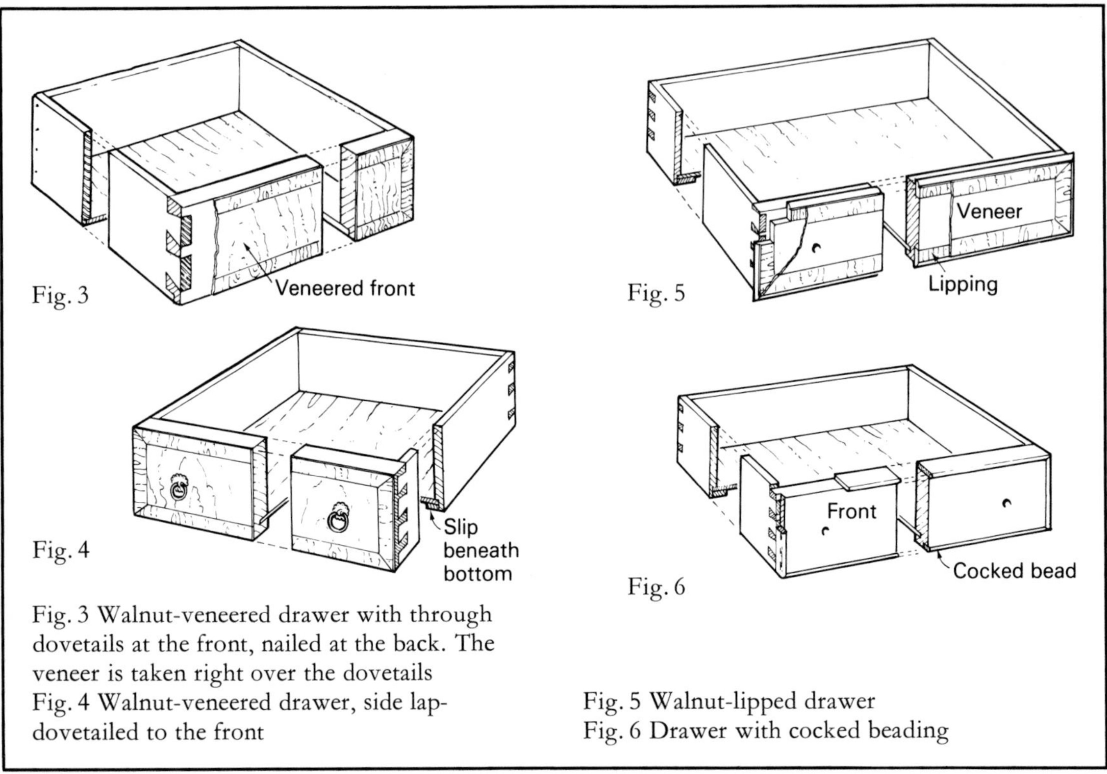

Fig. 3 Walnut-veneered drawer with through dovetails at the front, nailed at the back. The veneer is taken right over the dovetails
Fig. 4 Walnut-veneered drawer, side lap-dovetailed to the front

Fig. 5 Walnut-lipped drawer
Fig. 6 Drawer with cocked beading

Fig. 4 shows one of the methods used. There are rather coarse dovetails at the front and plain nailed butt joints at the back. The bottom is fitted into rebates in the front and sides, the grain running from front to back, but the method is rather unsatisfactory in that the bottom is liable to scrape as the drawer is moved because it is not set up at the back.

It was no doubt the realisation of this that prompted the idea of raising the bottom about $\frac{1}{4}$in. or so, and fitting slips of corresponding thickness beneath. This was successful up to a point, but seemed a somewhat crude arrangement in that both bottom and slips were visible at the sides. Furthermore the inevitable shrinkage either caused the bottom to pull in at the sides, or, as was more often the case, caused any joints in it to open. A rather better arrangement was that in Fig. 4, in which the sides were rebated to take both bottom and slips. It was certainly neater, but did not overcome the shrinkage problem. Anyone who owns a chest of the walnut period has no doubt found that the drawer bottoms have split or failed at the joints, though they may have been repaired subsequently.

A rather unusual way of overcoming the drawback of the bottom scraping is that used in the chest on page 18. Here the drawer fronts project downwards about $\frac{1}{4}$in. and the drawer runners behind drawer rails stand up $\frac{1}{4}$in., a method not often found.

It was during the walnut period that cabinet-making skills developed, and with them an element of standardisation in construction. Dovetails became finer and were not taken right through at the front but were stopped (lapped-dovetails) so that there was no end grain at the front over which veneer had to be laid. This is shown in Fig. 4.

A fashion that arose in the mid-walnut period was that of rebating the drawer front so that it stood forward from the general face of the carcase, as in Fig. 5. Whether this was an

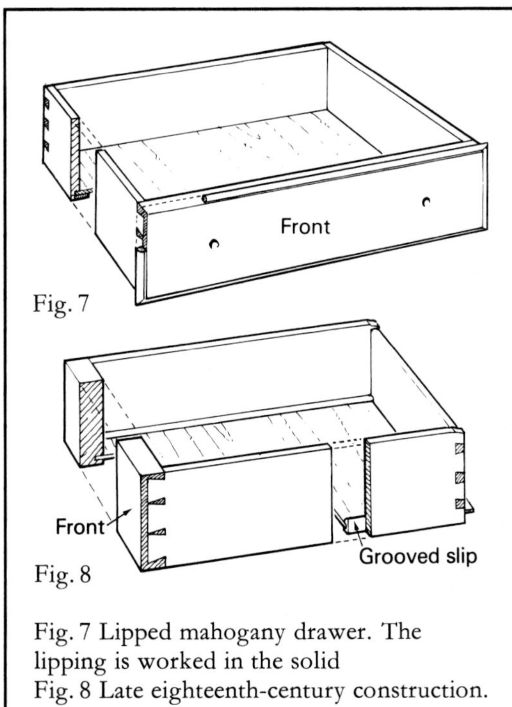

Fig. 7 Lipped mahogany drawer. The lipping is worked in the solid
Fig. 8 Late eighteenth-century construction. The grain of the bottom runs from side to side

attempt to make the drawers more dustproof, or just an idea to enhance the appearance, is something that cannot be proved. It was not universal, in any case; some drawers continued to be made flush with plain edges, and others with a cocked bead fitted around, as in Fig. 6. Since the raised drawer (lipped drawer as it is termed) was moulded around the edges, the moulding had to follow the fashion of having cross-grain. It was therefore necessary to work a rebate around the drawer front, glue in pieces of cross-grained walnut, veneer the face and finally work the moulding, generally a plain ovolo. This is shown clearly in Fig. 5. It was an effective enough treatment, but had the one disadvantage that the projecting moulding acted as a stop for the drawer, and with continual use it was liable to be knocked forwards, which necessarily affected the veneer on the face. Any practical restorer knows that this can involve an expensive repair.

In fact this type of lipped drawer was continued into the mahogany period, but by then the fronts were frequently in solid mahogany, the lipping being worked in the solid wood, and there was no longer any risk of damage as was the case when cross-grain walnut strips had to be applied. Fig. 7 shows this type.

Although some country-made chests had rather crude jointing, methods of construction in towns had largely been standardised by the early eighteenth century, and this was reflected in the drawers. Dovetails were fine and neat, those at the front being stopped (or lapped as it is called), the pins running almost to a point. At the back the dovetails were taken right through, the bottom fitting beneath the back. There was still, however, the rather unsatisfactory method of fitting the bottom into rebates in the sides, with slips beneath, although the fronts were grooved to receive it. Grain ran from front to back, and the weakness of this type of construction was that with shrinkage, any joints in the bottom invariably opened, because the sides of the bottom were fixed in their rebates. It was not until the end of the eighteenth century that a better form of construction was evolved. In this, grooved slips were glued inside the sides, the bottom being fitted dry in these and entering a groove in the front. The grain ran from side to side and passed beneath the back, and so the bottom was free to draw out of the groove in the front when shrinkage occurred, and there was no danger of its splitting. It was customary to allow the bottom to project about ¼in. at the back so that when shrinkage did occur the bottom could be pushed forward into the groove and be refixed with nails or screws (see Fig. 8). Another advantage was that the addition of the grooved slips gave increased thickness to the sides, making them better able to withstand wear. This method of construction has been maintained ever since, and is still used today in hand-made drawers. In the case of very small drawers, in which wear was negligible, the bottom was fitted flush into rebates in the sides and front, as in Fig. 9. Note the square member left at the bottom of the front dovetails so that the end of the rebate in the front is filled in.

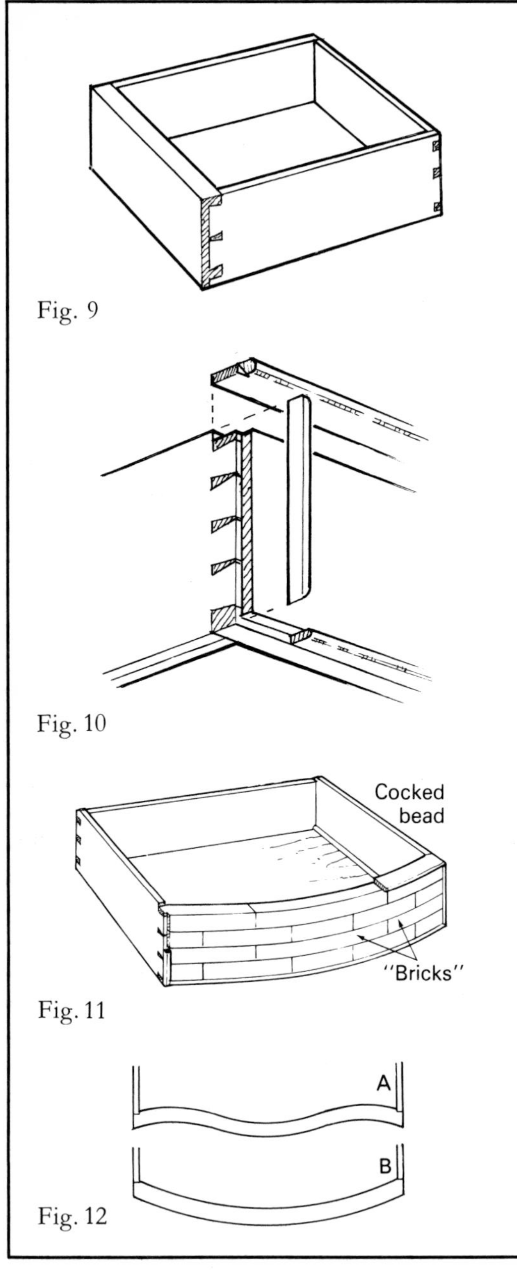

Fig. 9
Fig. 10
Fig. 11
Fig. 12

Fig. 9 Small drawer construction
Fig. 10 Cocked bead fitted around front
Fig. 11 Bow-fronted drawer built up with 'bricks'
Fig. 12 Shaped drawers. **A** serpentine; **B** bow

Mention had been made of cocked beads being fitted around drawer fronts as early as the late seventeenth century. This remained a popular feature throughout the eighteenth and nineteenth centuries, and is still used today. It was probably originally used as a protection for the edges of the veneer on the face of the drawer, as the edges are the most vulnerable parts. Fig. 10 shows such a drawer, and it will be seen that the front dovetails are curtailed so that the beads can fit in a rebate. At the top, the bead usually covered the entire thickness of the drawer front, as shown, but sometimes one finds drawers in which the rebate was continued along the top edge, as well as at the ends and the bottom.

Drawers with shaped fronts were often used in the eighteenth century. They might be either bow- or serpentine-shaped. Veneering was essential (except for very small drawers) and the usual method was to build the front by the 'brick' method, as in Fig. 11. Its advantage was that there was no excessive end grain, and it was not necessary to deep-cut a thick plank with the tremendous waste that would have involved. Vertical joints were staggered to ensure strength. To enable the dovetails to bed into square ends, small flats in alignment with each other were cut at the ends, as in Fig. 12. Apart from this, normal construction methods were used. Occasionally one comes across a small drawer laminated in its thickness. Several thin pieces were bent and glued around a shape former. An example of this is given on page 62.

Doors through the ages

There seems to be something rather obvious about the purpose of a door, yet the variety of ways in which doors have been made over the years is extraordinary. Of course, many considerations have to be taken into account, and perhaps the most important is the usage it would have to face. Contrast, for instance, the heavy, everyday wear of an oak cupboard door made in the sixteenth century with that of a delicate cabinet door intended for use in a polite drawing-room of the eighteenth century. The former might be opened a dozen or so times a day to reach everyday items needed in, say, the farmhouse kitchen or dining hall, whereas the other might be opened on an average perhaps once in a week to enable a book or possibly a piece of china to be withdrawn. Between these two there has been an almost endless variety of types.

Many early oak doors were merely slabs of solid wood, possibly pierced to give ventilation, or with carving on the face. It was the simplest form of construction but carried with it certain disadvantages, perhaps the chief of which was its liability to shrink or cast, though these drawbacks were minimised by the use of quarter-cut timber. Another serious disadvantage was the limitation imposed by the width in which the timber was available. If quarter-cut, it could be no wider than just under half the width of the log from which it was cut, because it would have been unwise to include the pith or centre of the log. If a wider door were needed it would have to be jointed and strengthened with battens fixed across the back. Another undesirable feature was the possibility of its splitting along the direction of the grain, especially if the door was pierced right through.

No doubt it was the realisation of these drawbacks that prompted the introduction of the framed and panelled door. It overcame all the disadvantages; shrinkage over the width was almost non-existent; strength in the width was ensured by the cross rails, and the width could be almost unlimited since it was only necessary to introduce muntins or intermediate uprights and fill in with narrow panels at each side. The framed door construction has remained in constant use ever since, though today it has to an extent been superseded by the use of plywood and blockboard.

However, the introduction of veneering in the later years of the seventeenth century and into the eighteenth century necessitated a different method, to enable veneer to be laid over a flat, flush surface, and this was continued at the same time as the framed method. It brought with it certain problems which were not always overcome successfully. These problems were almost entirely due to the inevitable movement of wood across the grain as moisture dried out. Admittedly people in those days were not in such a hurry as today and they left wood for as long as possible to season out. Even so there was always the possibility of shrinkage and the cabinet-makers were not always successful in their methods, as will be seen later.

An early solid slab door is shown in Fig. 1. It is about 12in. wide and, assuming that the wood was left to season beforehand, shrinkage would not have been excessive. It is, however, somewhat crude and might easily have warped out of shape, to say nothing of the weakness due to the piercing. Furthermore, to have any reasonable strength it would have to be fairly thick, and the result would be a somewhat heavy, clumsy door at best. The piercing is of a Gothic tracery design and there is a simple channel moulding cut with the chisel. It is from a food cupboard and is made of a single piece of oak. It has suffered from woodworm attack but is otherwise sound and has remained quite flat. Such a door was suitable enough for the early oak period but would have been entirely out of place in a delicate piece of furniture of a later period.

An example of an early framed door is that in Fig. 2. It is put together with mortise and tenon joints with a row of spindles, these having dowels turned at the ends to fit into holes in the rails. Most early turnings were done on the pole lathe; a length of cord was taken from the end of a springy lath or pole, around the wood to be turned, and down to a treadle. Only on the downward power stroke could turning be done, the turning tool being withdrawn as the pole sprang upward so reversing the rotation of the wood.

There are several features of special interest in the next example, Fig. 3. The craftsman has avoided all mitres at the meeting of the mouldings, and has thus been able to use two different mouldings, a chamfer, and a plain square edge. Whether he wanted to use different mouldings and realised that it would then be impossible to mitre them at the corners, or whether he wanted to avoid the complication of mitreing mouldings worked in the solid, and then discovered that with a few precautions he could finish the edges in almost any way, is debatable. Whatever the truth, the method had the advantage of simplicity since square shoulders could be cut at the tenons. The only exception is the tenon at the bottom of the centre muntin, and in reality this is really a square shoulder sloped at an angle to fit over the chamfer on the bottom rail, and is thus a form of scribe. On the main stiles are beads worked with the scratch-stock, these being stopped short of the rails so that a square edge was left against which the square shoulder of the rail could fit. As the lower edge of the top rail was left square, the moulded edges of the muntin merely butt against it, the shoulders of the tenon being left square.

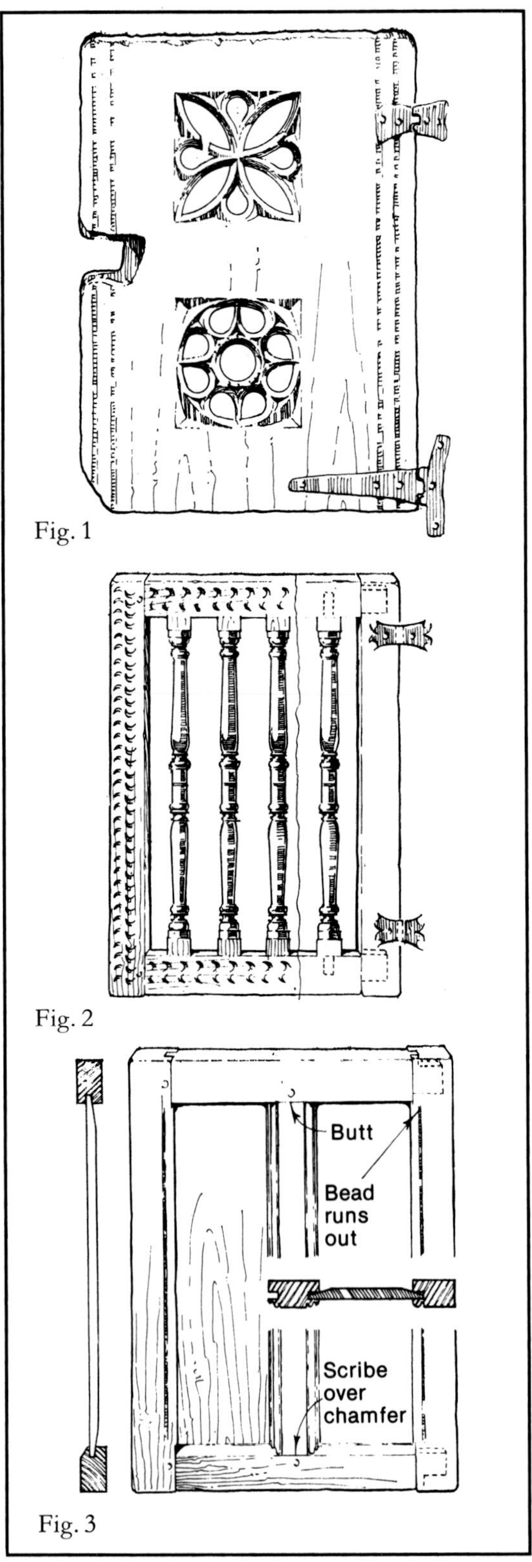

Fig. 1

Fig. 2

Fig. 3

A variation of the oak framed door is that in

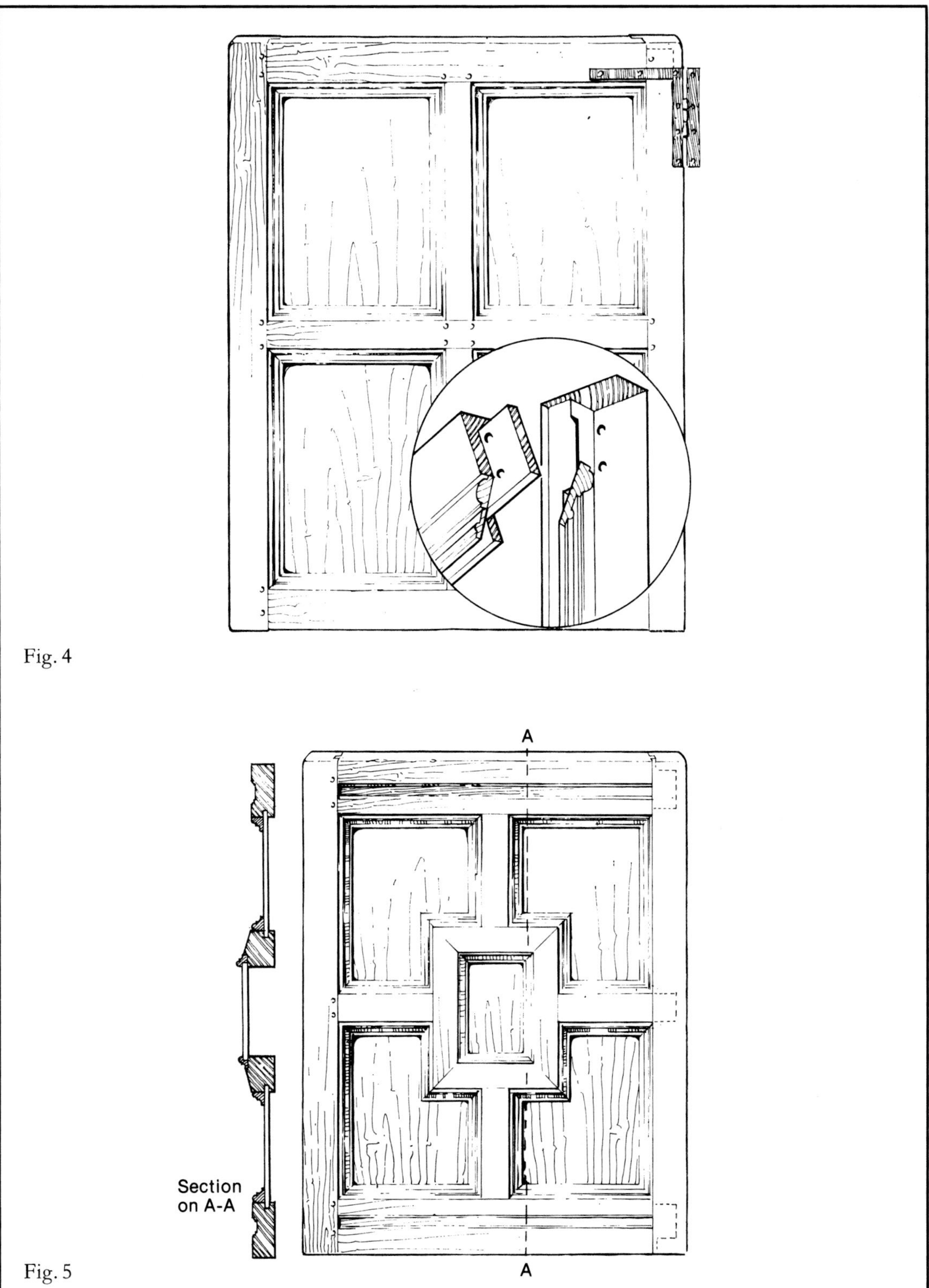

Fig. 4

Fig. 5

Fig. 4. The oak was mostly quarter cut, sometimes riven. The craftsman used the true mitre and overcame the problem of combining this with grooving to contain the panels. Note how the mortise is set in at the inside since the tenon is automatically cut away by the grooving. At the same time the tenon has long and short shoulders because the front of the stile has to be cut back level with the moulding which is worked in the solid. The whole thing was assembled without glue, the joints being pegged. Altogether it is a fine piece of woodwork.

Another example of a framed door is that in Fig. 5, but it differs from Fig. 4 in that the mouldings are not worked in the solid (stuck, as it was termed) but are applied in separate lengths mitred at the corners and glued to the framework. At the centre, the main members are mitred and rebated to take the small raised panel, a bolection moulding being fitted to hold it. Since the mouldings around the main framework are separate, all complications of combining the mitres with the joints are avoided. Frequently some quite elaborate patterns were built up, small oblong or triangular blocks being stuck to the framework and the mouldings mitred around these.

The introduction of veneering in the second half of the seventeenth century must have been a challenge to the craftsman. A wide flat surface was needed and it had to remain flat and have strength across the grain. One such door is that in Fig. 6, a long clockcase door. Top and bottom ends are clamped, and a strange feature is that the clamps are butted without any tongues. It seems a risky construction, but of course the veneer strengthens it considerably. Generally speaking this form of construction seems peculiar to the trade of clockcase-making.

Similar in construction is the clamped and veneered door in Fig. 7. The most usual construction was of pine with clamped ends, though sometimes it was framed with a flush panel glued in. The weakness in both cases was the liability of the panel to shrink, and this

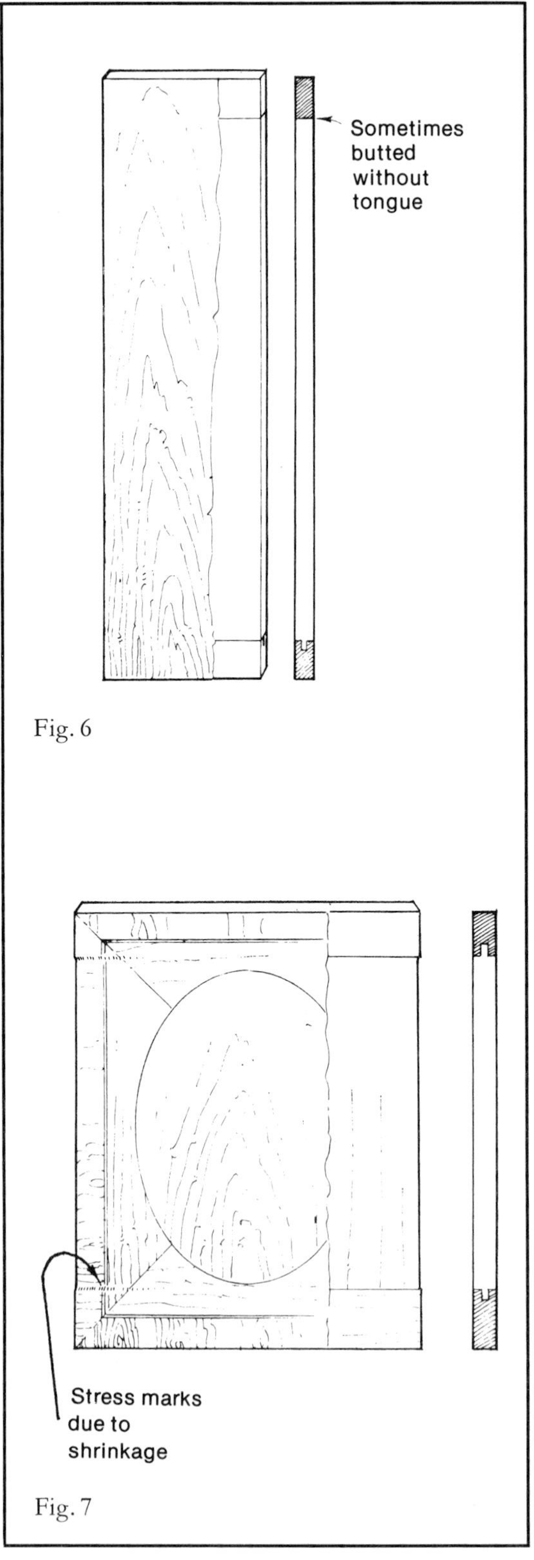

Fig. 6

Fig. 7

eventually showed itself either in stress marks in the veneer towards the edges as shown here, or in cracks towards the centre (sometimes both).

Although veneered flush doors were widely used in the early eighteenth century, the framed construction was sometimes preferred, but the general treatment was different from that of the oak period. The decorative value of cross veneering was realised, and thus we have the cross-veneered framed door in Fig. 8, with a separate panel held with a bolection moulding. The top moulding is shaped and may have been worked with the scratch-stock from a board in which the inner shape was sawn. After the rebate and the moulding had been worked, the outer shape would have been sawn, thus separating the moulding from the board. In this way the difficulty of gripping the moulding whilst it was being worked was overcome. Alternatively the moulding could have been turned as a complete circle and cut in two, enabling a pair of doors to be so treated. The wood would have been mounted on a flat backboard to enable it to be gripped by the face plate of the lathe. In this particular case the construction is rather unusual in that the top rail runs right through and has resulted in stress marks in the veneer, the consequence of shrinkage. In this example the veneer is mitred at the corners but frequently it was butted, with vertical joint lines.

From about 1725 the use of walnut was superseded by mahogany. This early mahogany was of the dark Cuban variety which, although frequently having magnificent figure, did not have the varied light and dark markings of walnut. The use of cross-veneering was therefore largely discontinued because it would not have shown up clearly as in the case of walnut. Consequently there was a return to the framed construction. Simpler examples had a plain square frame with thumb moulding around the edges and containing a fielded or raised panel. An elaboration of this is that in Fig. 9, a costly door to make by hand methods. A square-edged frame would be made first and

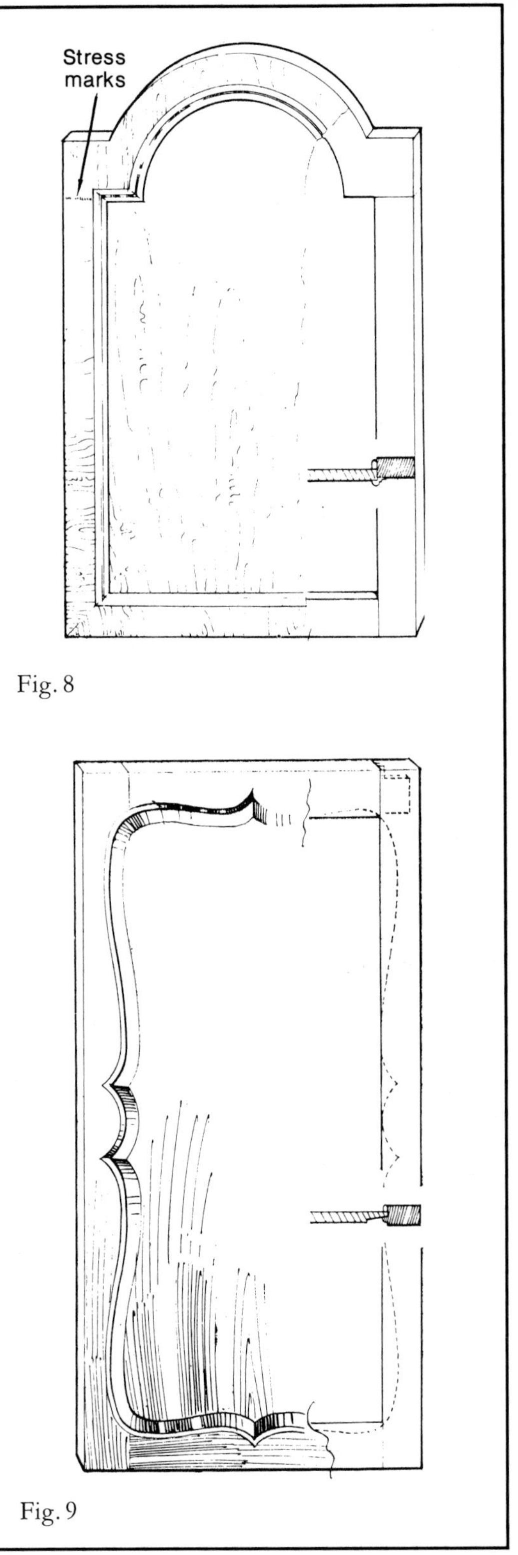

Fig. 8

Fig. 9

assembled dry and the inner shape bow-sawn. The rebate would have been largely chiselled, and the scratch-stock used for the moulding, though the carver would have to finish off the sharp inner corners. The fielding of the panel again would need the scratch-stock.

A variation of this is the door in Fig. 10 in which the top curve is formed by making the top rail extra wide and packing the stiles locally, cutting the shape afterwards and veneering. The moulding would either be made up separately and applied, or worked in the solid. In the latter case the whole thing would have to be in solid mahogany, or a local edging of mahogany would be applied. Lower quadrant corners would be set in separately.

Perhaps the most characteristic door of the eighteenth century was the lattice or barred door of which Fig. 11 is an example. The lattice moulding was usually of astragal section, about $\frac{3}{8}$in. wide, and in the best work the back was grooved to fit over $\frac{1}{8}$in. bars. The glass was either beaded or puttied in. Note that the section of the framework moulding is half that of the lattice. In all cases the mitre lines halve the over-all angle of the joining mouldings. Framework and lattice sections shown below.

Patterns of these lattice doors were manifold, the more elaborate designs involving shape mouldings. An example is that in Fig. 12. In making such a door the craftsman would assemble the framework and fit a flat panel to the rebate. On this the whole design would be marked out. He would then work the lattice mouldings with the scratch-stock at the edge of a board, the side of which he would have cut to the required shape. The moulding was then sawn away and fitted to the marked out panel. All the mitres halve the over-all angle, and in assembling, only the mitres were glued. He would then remove the panel, turn the whole frame upside-down, and add the stiffening bars at the back, these being checked into the framework where required. Thin strong canvas glued to the joints in the bars strengthened them.

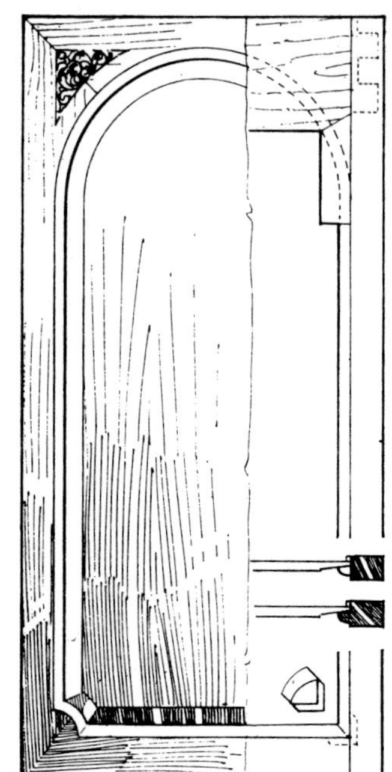

Fig. 10

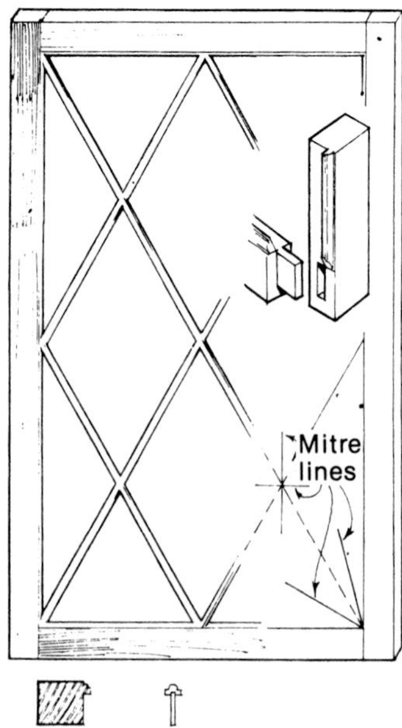

Fig. 11

The finest eighteenth-century furniture frequently involved shaped work and this was always expensive. It was not merely that it cut into a lot of wood, though this was costly in itself, but that the work involved was far greater than in straight work. An example of a framed bow-front door is that in Fig. 13. The framework is rebated and moulded to receive the panel, an essential feature being that the stile rebates are parallel so that the panel can be added after assembly.

Fig. 14 is the flush counterpart of the bow door. Usual construction was to cooper the door, that is to glue strips of wood about 2in. wide side by side, the edges being at a slight angle to allow for the curve. Veneering followed, and in the best work both sides were covered, though on many old pieces only the face side was veneered. This coopered method was also used for doors of serpentine shape.

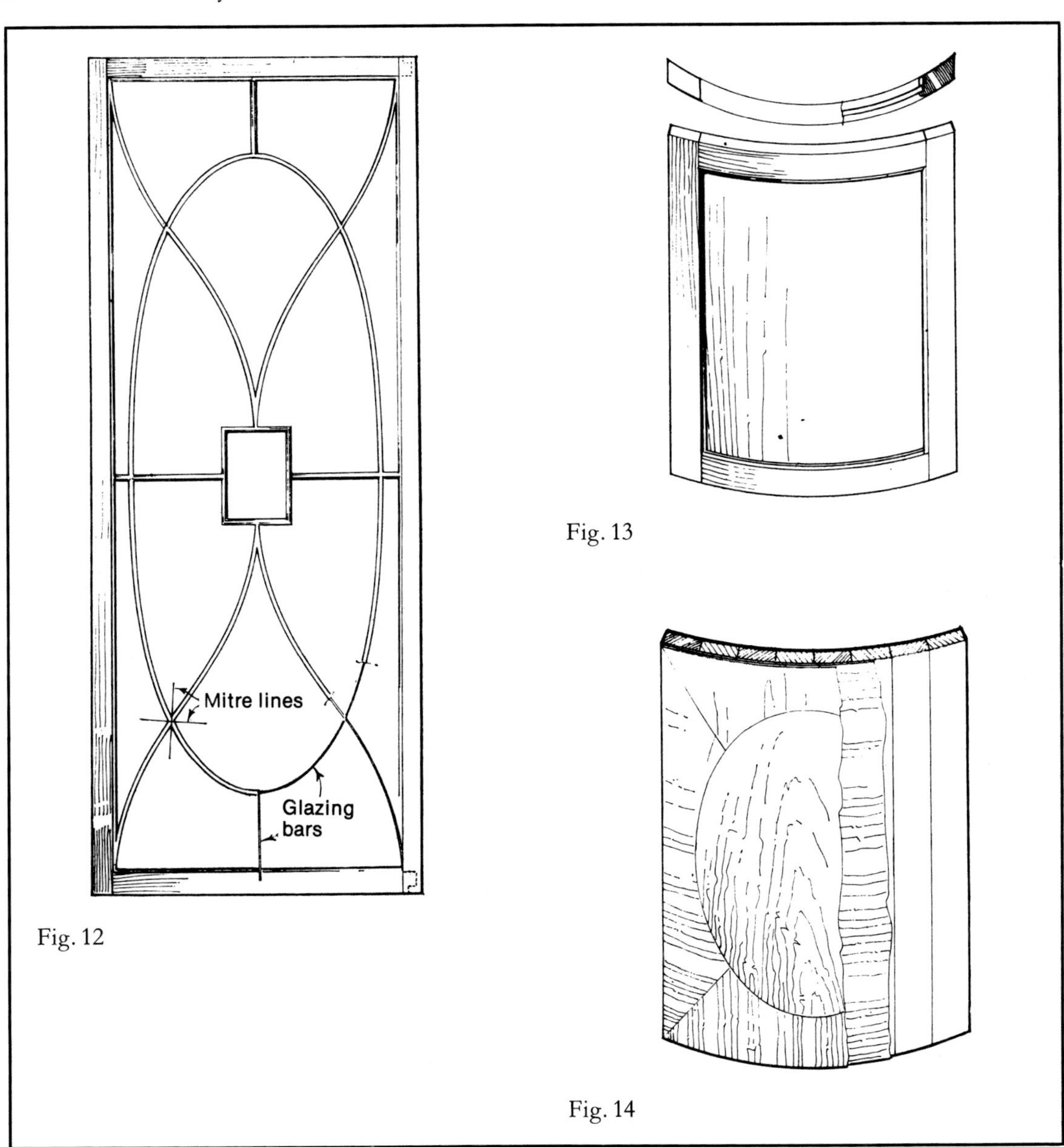

Fig. 12

Fig. 13

Fig. 14

Mouldings and their origins

Little domestic furniture of a date earlier than the sixteenth century has survived, and such early woodwork that has come down to us in the form of screens and fittings for churches, halls and so on is essentially Gothic in character. It was during the sixteenth century that that intangible influence known as the Renaissance swept through the land. At first it was barely understood and frequently had little more effect than the application of a few motifs grafted on to a Gothic groundwork. Renaissance details were derived from ancient Greek and Roman buildings, and mouldings in particular lent themselves to application to furniture, though at first the sixteenth-century craftsman made very free copies of the originals often mixing classical with Gothic styles.

In any case it has to be realised that to copy exactly on a small scale the mouldings of a huge Greek or Roman temple would not have been practicable. Sections had to be adapted, partly to suit the reduced scale, and also to suit the different technique required for working in wood as opposed to stone.

Here it is worth while considering the technique followed in working mouldings in wood. One or more of the following tools would be used, the moulding plane, the scratch-stock or carving tools. Of these methods, the first required that the craftsman had suitable moulding planes, and in the early days, at any rate, he frequently had none. He then had either to work the moulding with carving tools or use the scratch-stock.

The scratch-stock is shown in Fig. 1 and consists of a notched block of wood cut through the middle and held together with screws, the cutter being held between the two pieces. In use, it was worked back and forth along the wood, the notch bearing against the edge. It had the great advantage of simplicity since the tool itself was easily made and its cutter was just a thin piece of steel filed to a reverse of the required section. Since the edge was filed straight across, it could be used in

Fig. 1

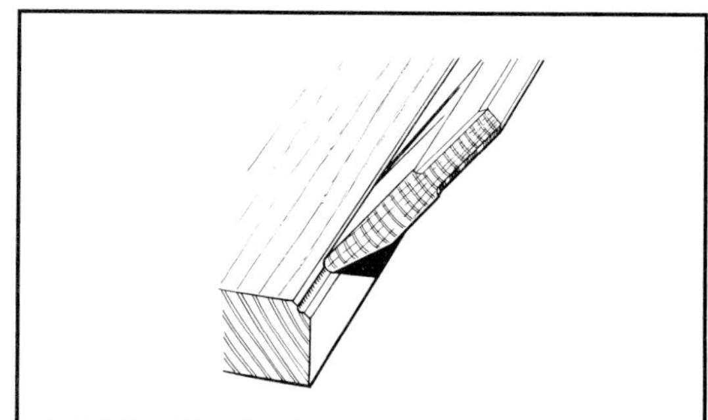

Fig. 2

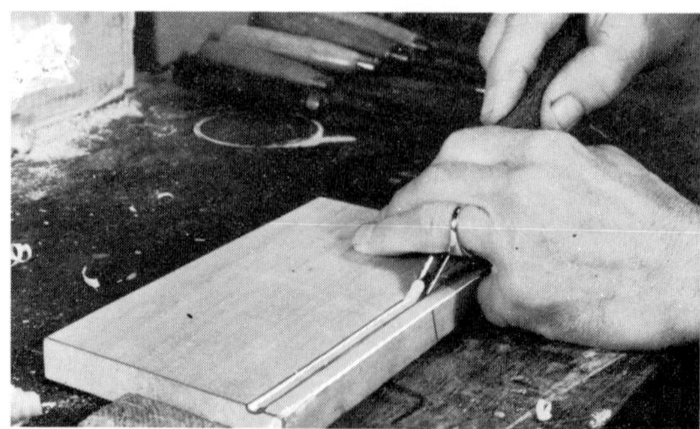

Fig. 3

either direction to suit the grain of the wood. Furthermore it could be stopped at any particular point or be run out gradually.

This is in contrast with the moulding plane which must be taken along the entire edge of wood, Fig. 2, without being stopped. This, of course, was because of its straight, flat sole. On the other hand, the scratch-stock was laborious in use and was suitable, therefore, only for small mouldings, unless the section were such that the bulk of the waste could be removed with the ordinary bench plane first, leaving the scratch-stock to finish off and so ensure the same section being maintained throughout.

Reverting for a moment to the use of carving tools for working a moulding, one does sometimes come across a section which is so irregular along its length that it is obvious that neither moulding plane nor scratch-stock could have been used. If the section were rounded the likelihood is that a rebate plane was used and the resulting facets taken out by using glasspaper or its equivalent. But a hollow section would have had to be cut with a carving tool if neither plane nor scratch-stock were available. Fig. 3 shows the carving tool in use, though it was seldom that this method was used because of its being too laborious and because of the irregularity involved.

By the eighteenth century the making of moulding planes had become an established trade, and a large range of patterns became available. It is doubtful, however, whether the employed cabinet-maker himself ever had much in the way of moulding planes. The space they would take up would largely preclude the possibility of every cabinet-maker in a large workshop having a full set of planes. In any case he could not have afforded such a set of planes, and there would also be the difficulty of removing them from shop to shop if he changed his job. The individual workman may have had a few basic moulding planes but the probability is that in a large shop the master cabinet-maker had the necessary planes which the employees would use.

I recall in my early days in the workshop that most cabinet-makers kept a $\frac{1}{8}$in. bead plane for working along the edges of shelves, for the hingeing edge of a door where it continued the line of the hinge knuckle, or for making cocked beads for drawers, the reason being that it would not have been economical for the machinist to set up a spindle moulder specially for so simple a job. Some men also had one or two round planes for working hollow sections, especially those engaged in repair work. Generally, however, the main run of mouldings were machined.

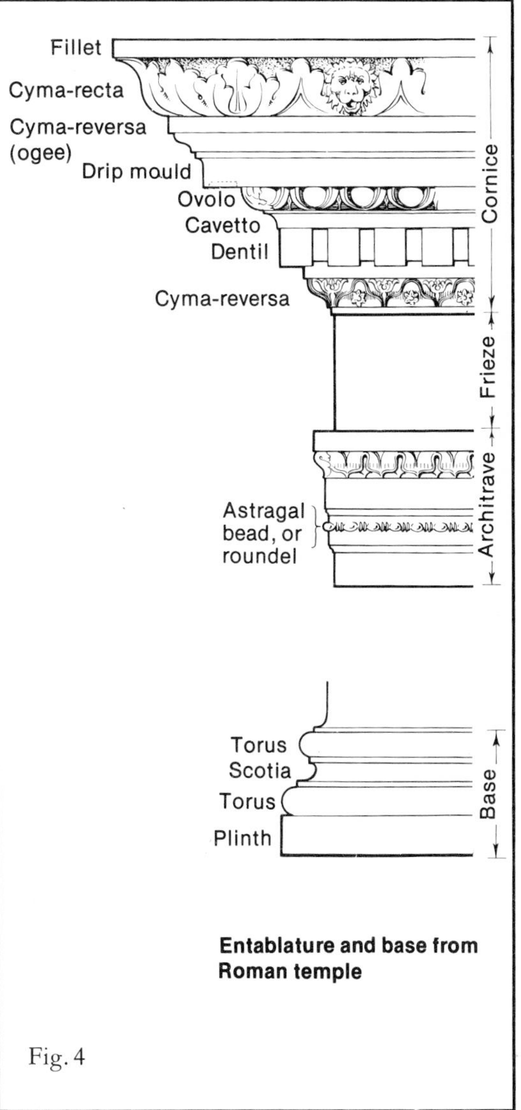

Entablature and base from Roman temple

Fig. 4

Sections of eighteenth-century mouldings were invariably based on the classical, but as already mentioned, were adapted for working in wood. Fig. 4 shows a portion of the entablature and base of a Roman temple, and Fig. 5 gives individual sections. Generally Greek shapes were based on elliptical and freehand curves whereas the Romans preferred shapes based on the circle.

Some actual sections used by the eighteenth-century woodworkers are given in Fig. 6, and it will be seen that all the members of a large moulding were taken from the small individual sections or combinations of them. A point to be realised is that in the case of large cornice and other mouldings such as those given in Fig. 7, nearly all the members were worked individually. It would not have been practicable to use a single moulding plane for working the whole section of a large moulding. For one thing the effort required for using so large a plane would have been too great. Furthermore, the varying direction of grain in wood might

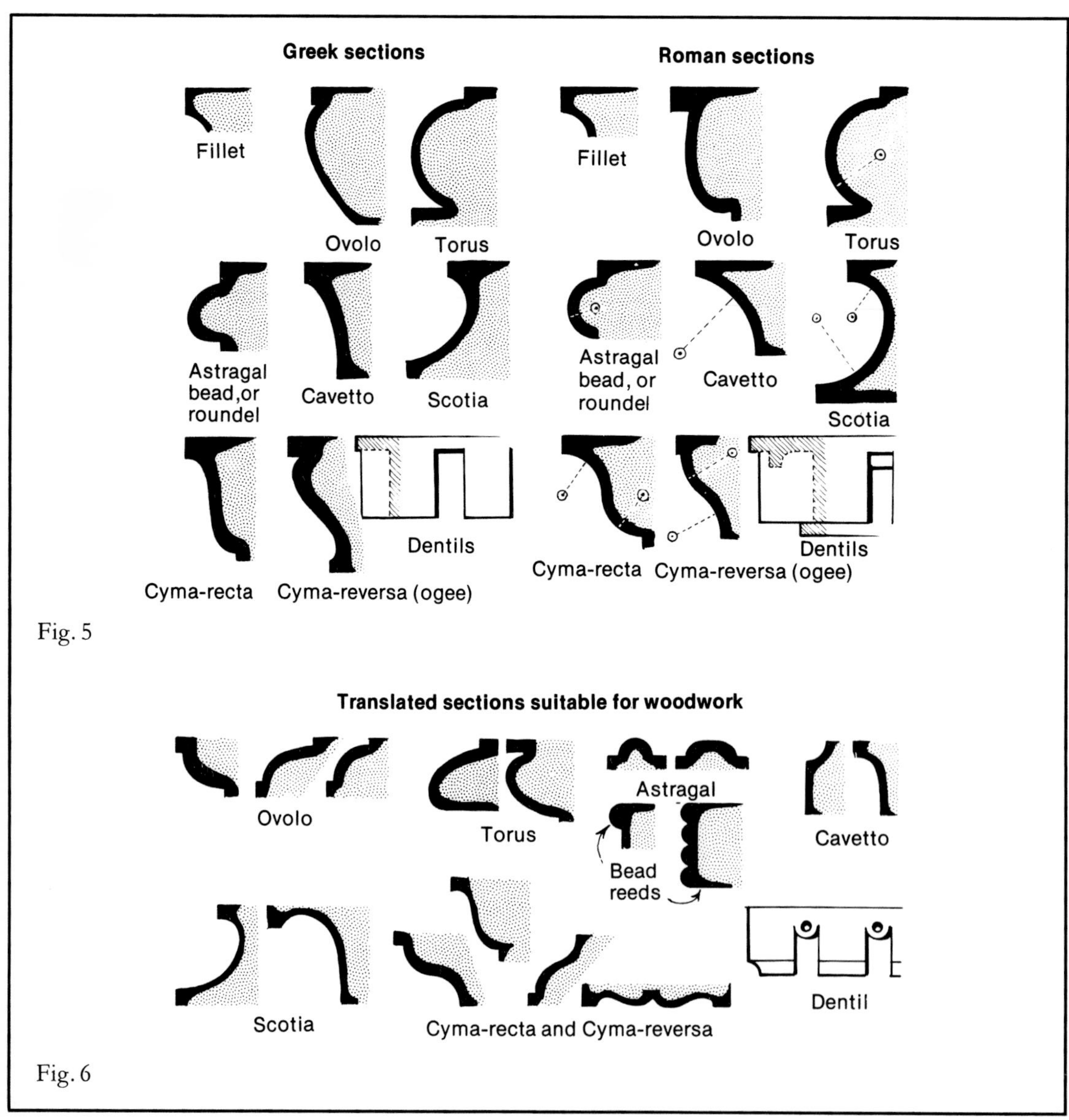

Fig. 5

Fig. 6

easily have resulted in some members tearing out in the grain although there might be no difficulty with other parts. Another point is that most such large mouldings were backed with softwood, the facing of hardwood being just sufficient to enable the section to be worked. For practical reasons a single plane to work the whole could not have been used. The subject is developed more fully in my book *Antique or Fake?* where the method of working mouldings is explained more fully.

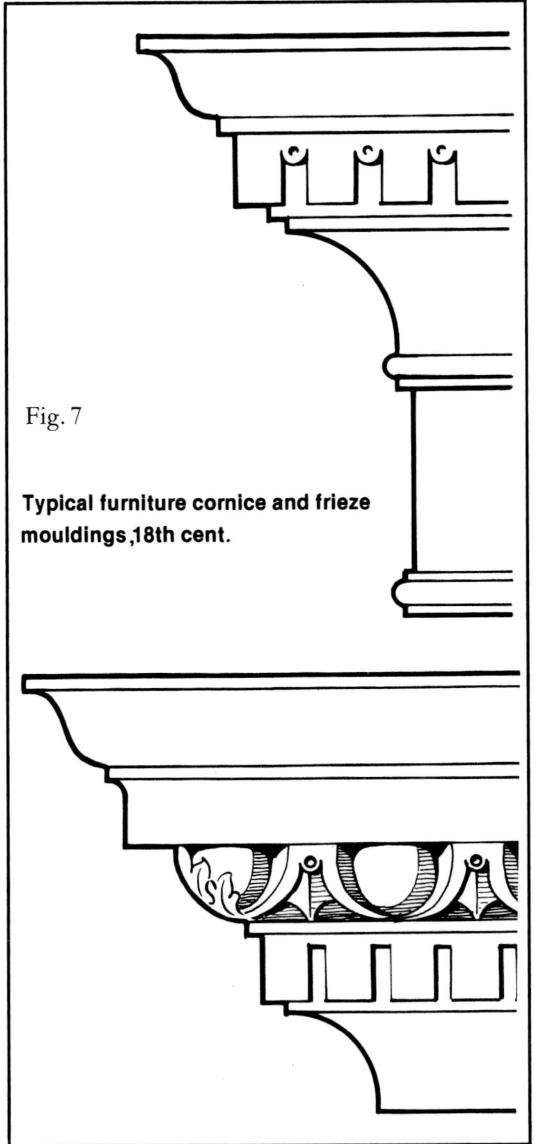
Fig. 7

Typical furniture cornice and frieze mouldings,18th cent.

Making drawings of old furniture

I am sometimes asked about the method I follow in preparing drawings of old pieces of furniture. Well, in the first place the finished drawings are never done when the item is being measured. All that is needed in the first place are sketches showing front elevation, side elevation and plan, with all measurements noted. Usually the sketches are quite rough with no attempt at giving correct proportions, but that does not matter providing all essential sizes are noted. It would not be practicable to complete the drawings to scale when measuring, because drawings for publication have to be finished in ink, and for this, it is essential to work at a table with a good light, and as a rule neither is possible in the place where the item stands. In any case it takes quite a long time to complete a finished drawing, and it would not be possible to spend so long in the house, museum or gallery where the piece is.

When making the finished drawing, all that is necessary is to use a scale and, following the sizes noted, the exact proportions of the item can be reproduced. It is, of course, necessary to note all essential sizes, including thicknesses of timber, dimensions of drawers, cupboards, inlay lines and bandings, etc. Furthermore moulding sections have to be copied, generally in full size. For this a piece of card can sometimes be held at the end of the moulding, and a pencil drawn around the contour, as in Fig. 1, but allowance has to be made for edges or corners which have become rounded with wear. When this method is not possible either the various members have to be measured individually, or a pack of cards can be pressed against the moulding as in Fig. 2, though it is possible to obtain a special template (the Maco) which works on the same principle using a pack of metal strips.

Sometimes small details such as frets or other shaped items can be copied by holding a card at the back and drawing around the shape much as in Fig. 1. This, of course, is impossible with inlay details, and close copying with sizes noted is the alternative, though sometimes tracing paper can be used.

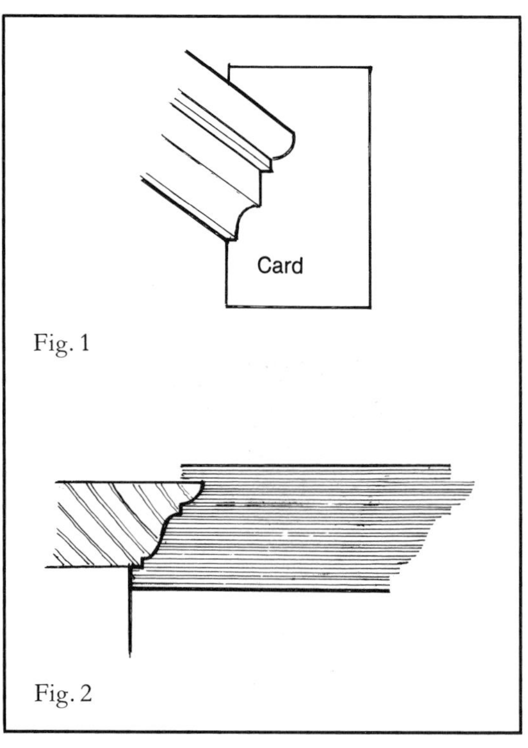

Fig. 1

Fig. 2

Fig. 3 Chair in carved and inlaid mahogany, about 1775 (Victoria and Albert Museum).

An invaluable general help is a rigid three-foot rule, not so much for measuring, but rather for offering against shaped parts so that the degree of curvature can be noted, using a separate rule, as in Fig. 4. In this way the rake of a chair back or the dishing of a curve can be noted.

The matter is more complicated when an item has compound curvature, that is, when it is shaped in both front and side elevation (and sometimes also in plan). Quite often a drawing of a part has to be made at an angle which is somewhere between front and side elevation. In such cases I find it invaluable to ascertain the section of timber from which the part was cut. All timber in its original conversion is cut to a rectangular section, whether actual squares or flat boards, and the craftsman has had to win his shapes from them. This is specially applicable to chairs. For instance, take the chair in Fig. 3, in which there is scarcely a single straight line in the whole thing. Yet all the shapes had to be cut from straight timber of rectangular section. Consider the back legs. To be able to make a scale drawing of the back leg it is necessary to imagine the timber from

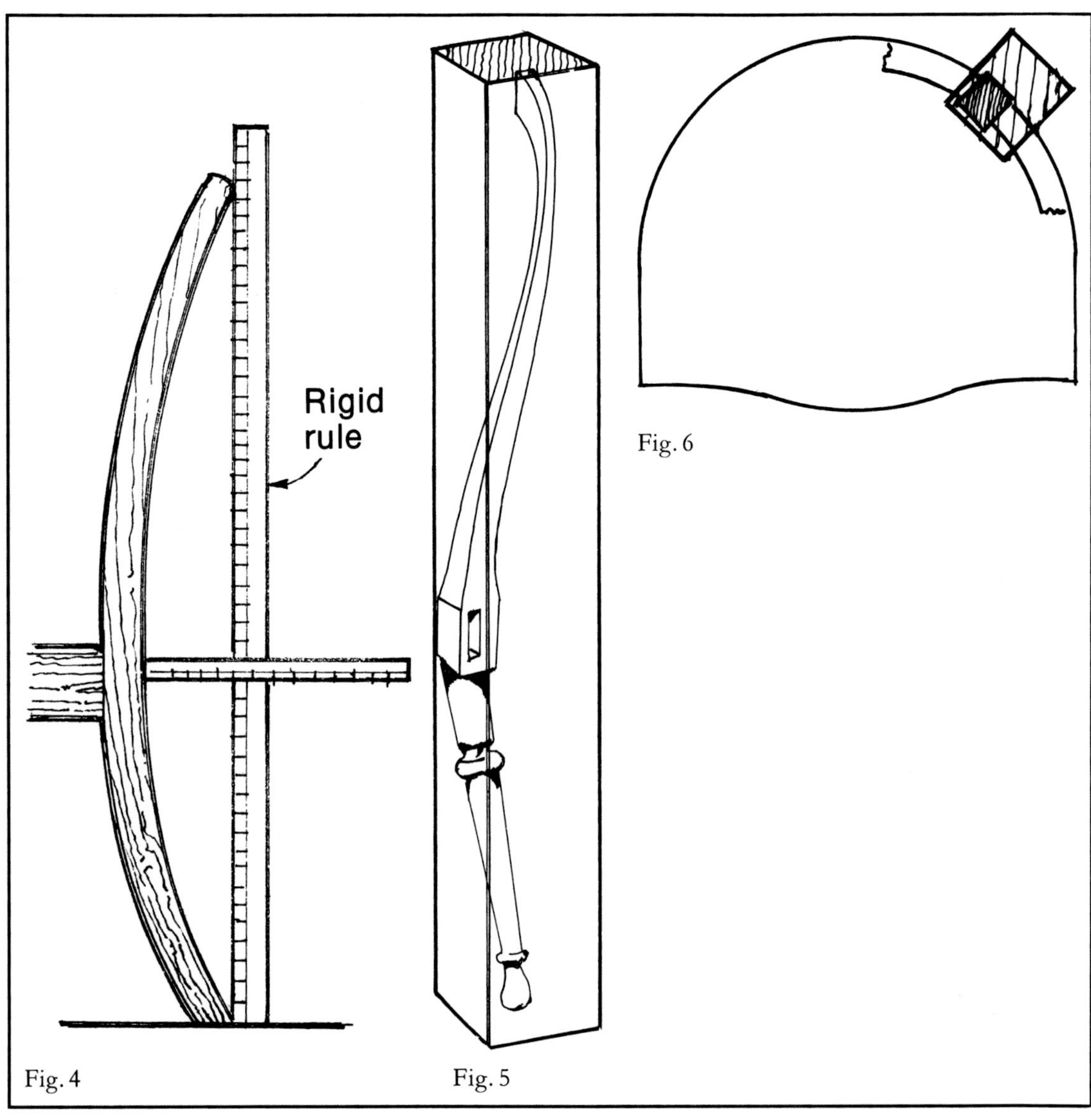

Fig. 4

Fig. 5

Fig. 6

which it was cut. The idea is explained in Fig. 5 and 6. In addition to the front oval shape it also has the backward rake. Furthermore, the back is also curved in plan. To enable the complicated shape to be drawn, the flat sectioned timber from which it was cut would have to be drawn in at an angle as in Fig. 6. By working in this way it is possible to follow the method used by the chairmaker, and to realise the practical way in which he solved the problem.

Another consideration applying to all pieces, shaped or straight, is that of construction, and it is invariably necessary to get underneath the piece to note the direction of joints etc. Sometimes it is impossible to be perfectly sure of details, short of dismantling the item, because they are hidden. Generally, however, one can form a shrewd idea of the method used – at any rate in eighteenth-century items and later, because methods of construction had largely become standardised by then (though the exception does turn up, as explained elsewhere in this book). Earlier work, especially country-made pieces, often pose some problems, and it can be intriguing to consider why the craftsman made the piece in the way he did.

Finished drawings for reproduction have to be in Indian ink but are first drawn in pencil with T square, set squares, compasses and various French curves in thin wood, plastic material or something similar. I always make my own curves, fretting them out and finishing with file and glasspaper. Over the years I have accumulated a large number of curves from which I can usually select what is needed, but when an odd shape does turn up, I make a fresh curve for it, as it will invariably come up again in the future. This, of course, applies only to the large shapes which would be difficult to draw cleanly with the pen freehand. Small curves present no difficulty and can be put in freehand. Incidentally, I use one of the special pens, such as the Rotring, for use with curves as there is no danger of a blot or smear being made at the edge of the curve as there would be if an ordinary pen were used. A blot or smear is awkward to deal with as it has to be erased or painted out with Snopake or something similar. Blots of this kind can be the cause of some appallingly blue language, especially if it happens on a nearly finished drawing.

For straight lines I use an ordinary pen against a straight-edge with a bevelled edge. And indeed I find the ordinary pen preferable to a ruling pen for general work because the thickness of lines can be varied at will. To my mind a drawing with all the lines of the same thickness can be very dull and uninteresting. By varying the thickness, emphasis can be given where desirable and the whole thing made to look attractive.

Glossary of terms

Astragal

Small bead moulding with fillet at each side (A). It may be grooved at the underside (B) to fit over the bars of a lattice door.

Backed moulding

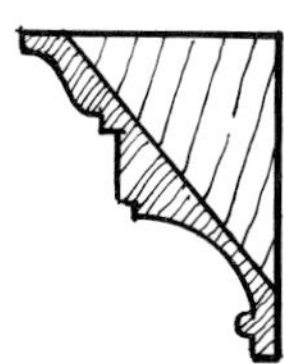

One which has a thin hardwood facing in which the section is worked, with softwood backing. Used mostly for cornice mouldings.

Back flap hinge

One used chiefly for bureau falls, etc. It is much wider than the butt hinge used for doors.

Bare-faced

Term applied to a tenon (A) or tongue (B) which has no shoulder at one side.

Bolection moulding

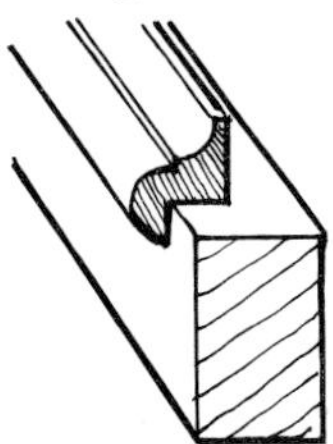

A rebated moulding fitting over the edge of a part so that it is raised and stands beyond the level of the general surface.

'Brick' method

System used in shaped work such as the drawer fronts of a bow- or serpentine-front chest of drawers. See page 98.

Bullnose plane

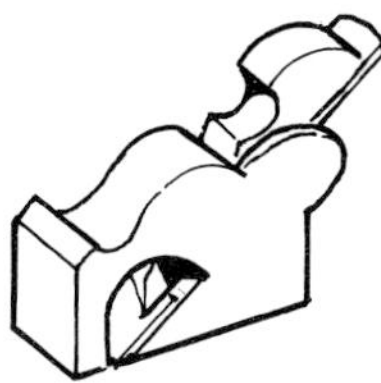

Small rebate or shoulder plane with the cutting edge near the front.

Case furniture

General term referring to items such as cupboards, wardrobes, etc. which are of box-like form as compared with tables, chairs, etc. which consist mostly of rails and legs.

Caul
A flat panel used to press veneer down on to the groundwork. Paper is interposed to prevent it from sticking, and, in the case of animal glue, is first heated to liquefy the glue. It is cramped down.

Chair-maker's scraper

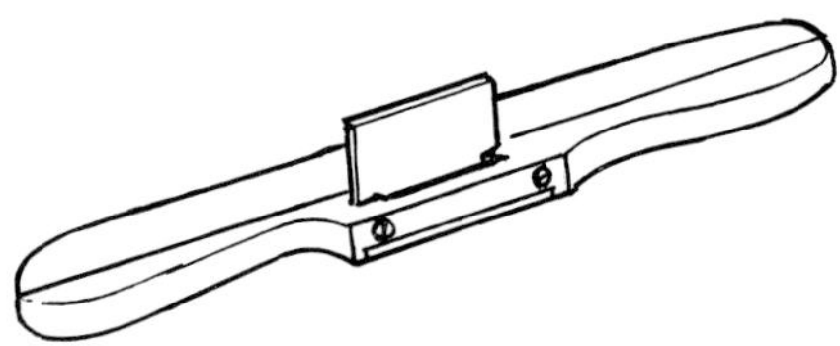

Tool used to finish the parts of a chair. Its cutter is set vertically and the edge is turned so that it scrapes rather than cuts, and therefore does not tear out the grain. The chair-maker has several of varying shapes to suit straight work and varying degrees of curvature.

Clamps

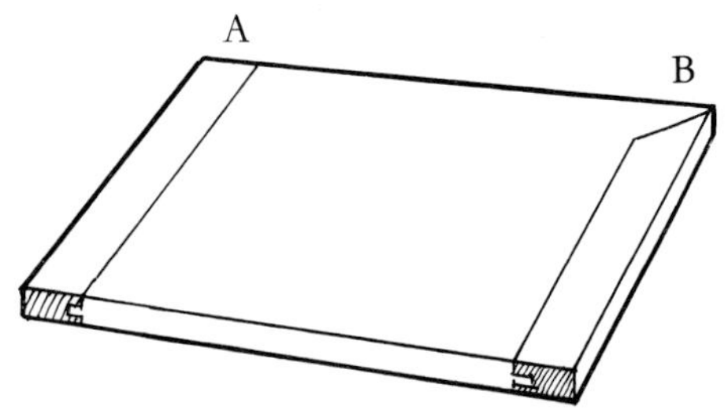

The cross pieces fitted to the ends of a panel such as a bureau fall to strengthen it across the grain. It is usually tongued on. It may run right through (A), or be mitred (B).

Cocked bead

A small bead, usually $\frac{1}{8}$in. thick projecting beyond the general face of the work and often fitted around drawer fronts and sometimes doors. Apart from its decorative value it serves to protect the edges of any veneer on the surface. It may occupy the whole thickness of the wood (A) or it may be let into a rebate (B).

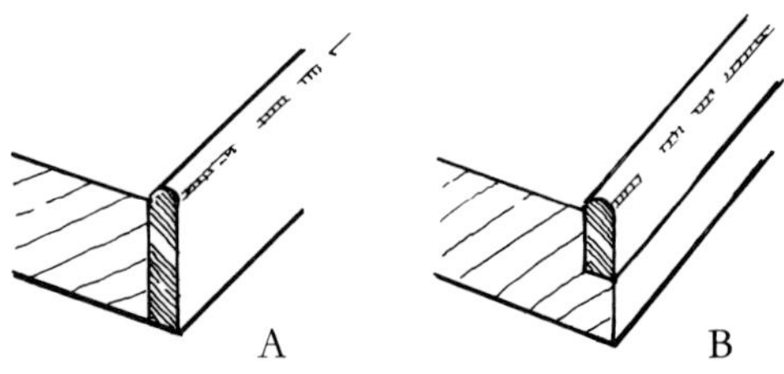

Coopered door

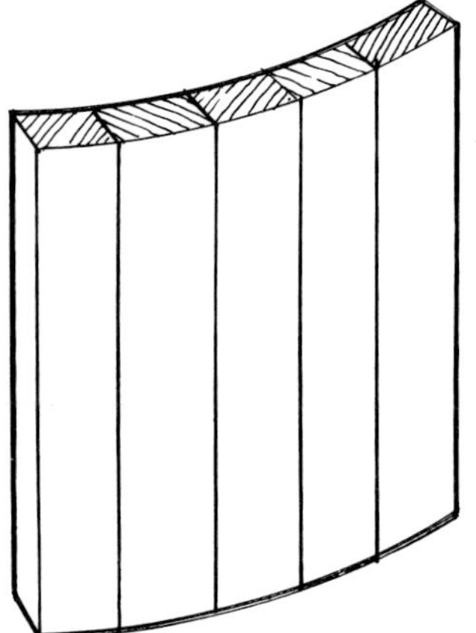

Form of construction used for some shaped doors and consisting of wood strips glued together side by side with canted joints to enable the shape to be worked. The surface is invariably veneered afterwards.

Counterbore

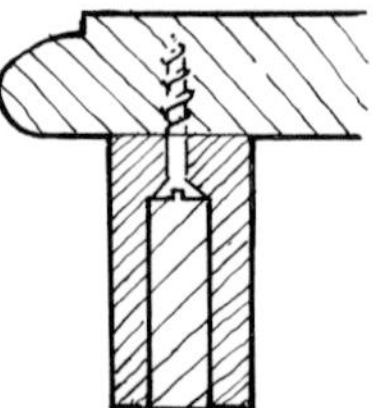

Device used in screwing a part such as a top through a deep rail to avoid using an unnecessarily long screw. The hole in the rail is slightly larger than the screw head.

Cross peen

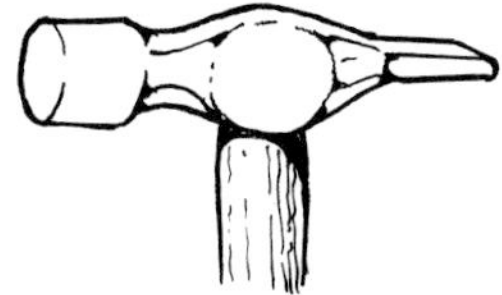

The flat back part of a Warrington or London pattern hammer. Apart from starting small nails, the cross peen is used by cabinet-makers to press down small inlay bandings and lines.

Door, parts of

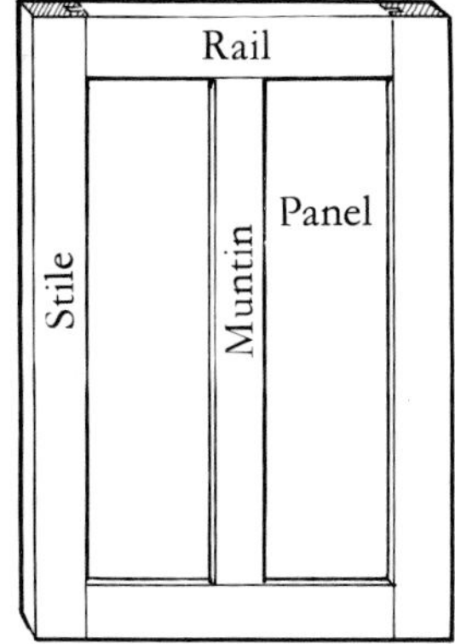

The chief parts of a framed door are shown in the illustration.

Dovetails

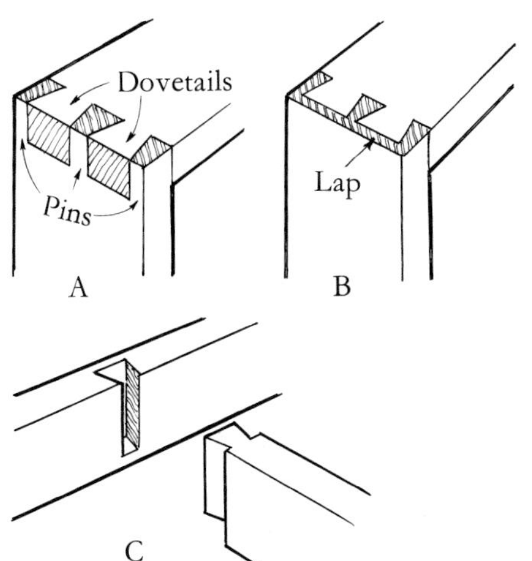

Chief types are the through (A), lapped (B), and slot (C). There are many variations of each.

Fielded panel

One with a wide decorative rebate (usually canted) worked around the front edges. It gives a raised effect and enables a thick panel to be fitted to the narrow grooves in the framework.

Gesso

Foundation preparation used in gilding, consisting chiefly of gilder's whiting and parchment cutting size or rabbit skin glue.

Glue block

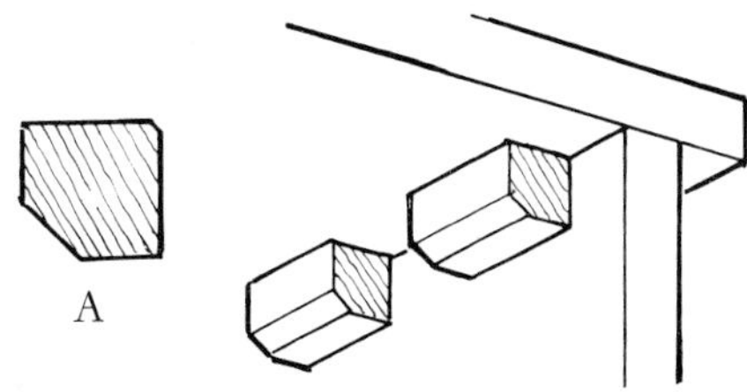

Small softwood block with two adjacent sides at right angles and bevelled at the outer corner (A). The extreme inner corner is also taken off to ensure that it beds down into the corner angle. Used to strengthen parts fitted together at right angles. After gluing it is rubbed back and forth once or twice to ensure close contact.

Halved joint

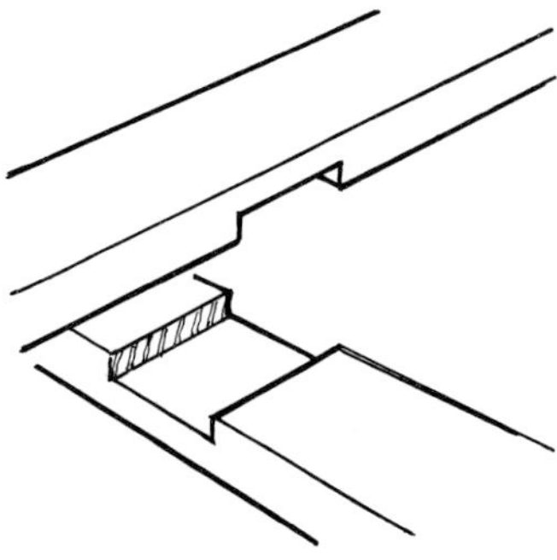

One used to join parts together in a cross, L, or T formation. Each part is cut away to half its thickness.

Hammer veneering

Method used in which the veneer is pressed down and surplus glue squeezed out by working the veneering hammer (q.v.) zigzag fashion over the surface.

Haunch

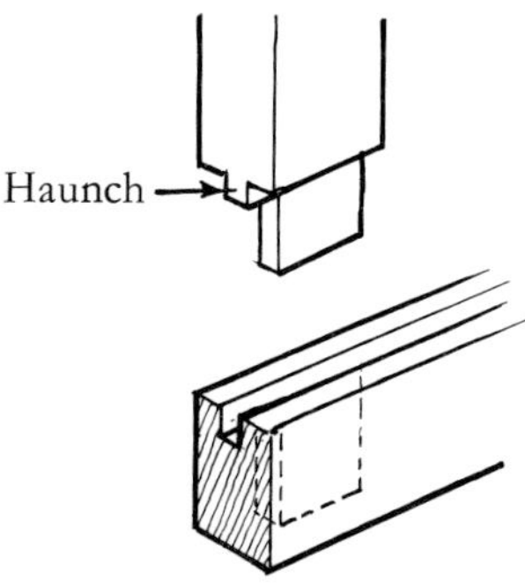

Small projection at the side of a tenon, usually to fill in the groove in the mortised part.

Kicker

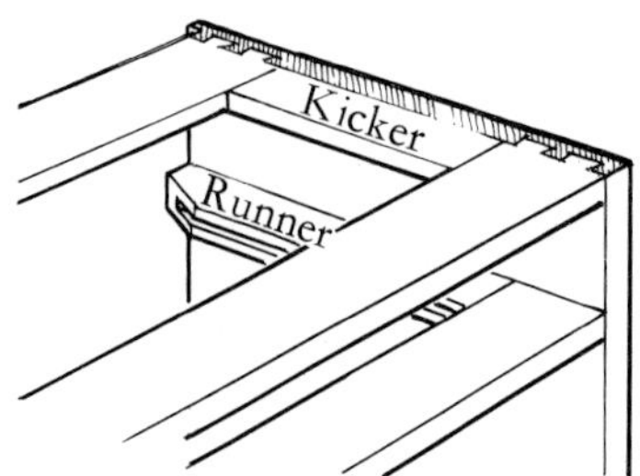

The corresponding part to a drawer runner fitted above a drawer to prevent it from dropping as it is opened.

Knuckle joint

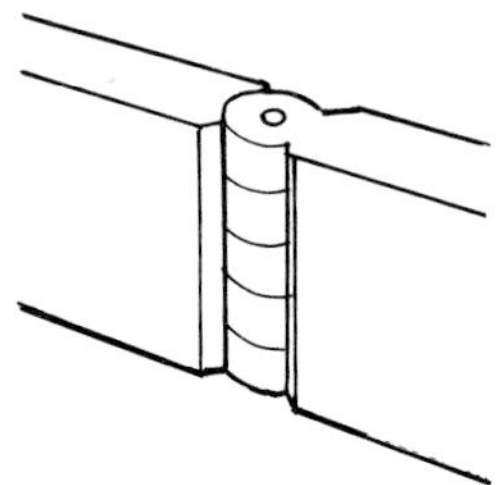

One used to pivot a fly leg to the main framework.

Lapped dovetail

See Dovetail.

Lipped drawer

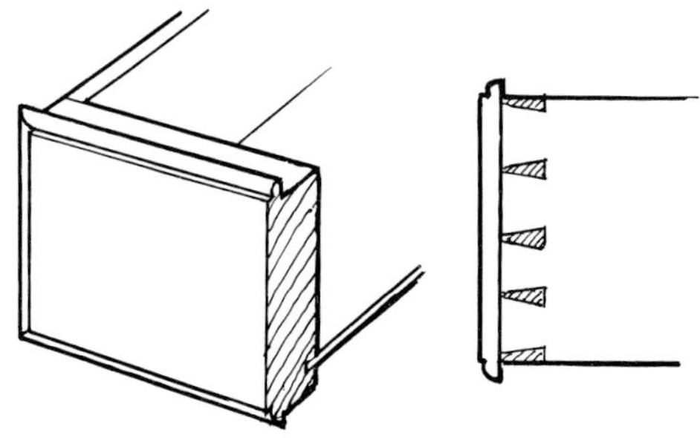

One in which the front is rebated all round at the inside edges.

Marquetry

A form of inlay carried out in veneer.

Moulding box

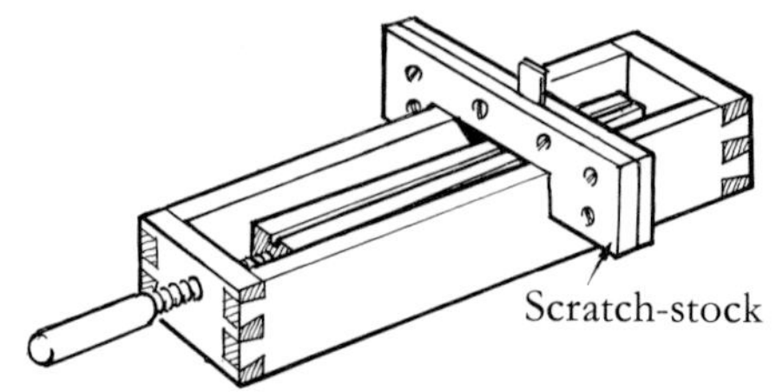

Apparatus used in conjunction with a scratch-stock for working a moulding or groove along a tapered or turned leg. The upper surface of the latter is positioned in height so that it is in the same plane as the top of the box and is held laterally so that the required moulding or groove is parallel with the box sides.

Muntin
See Door, parts of.

Oil gilt
Form of gilding in which the gold leaf is held by the tackiness of a coat of gold size which is oil-based. It is not capable of the highly burnished finish of water-gilding (q.v.).

Old woman's tooth

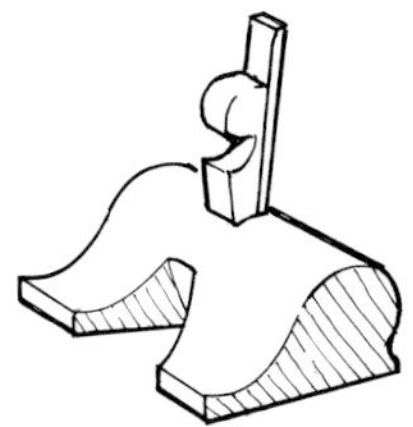

A router with the cutter set at a high angle in a wooden stock. Used for finishing a recess to equal depth throughout.

Pelleting

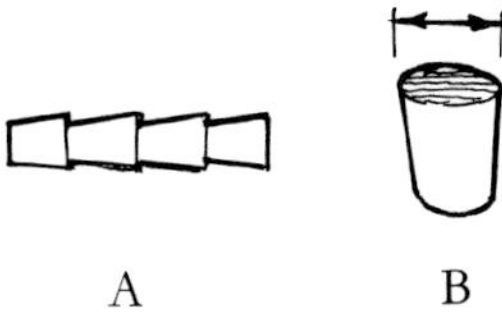

A method of filling in the hole of a counter-bored screw. Pellets are tapered in length and are turned with the grain running crosswise (B). Usually half a dozen or so are turned in a single length as at (A) then cross-cut. When glued into the hole the grain runs in the same direction as that of the surrounding wood.

Pins
See under Dovetail.

Plough plane

Tool used to cut grooves. It has several cutters of varying widths and there is an adjustable fence and depth stop.

Quarter-cut

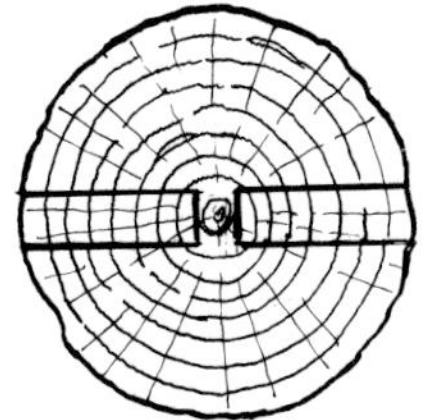

Timber so converted that the boards are sawn radially to the log. Such timber is stable and in the case of oak, beech, and some other woods exhibits the rays or characteristic flower or figure.

Rail
See Door, parts of.

Rule joint

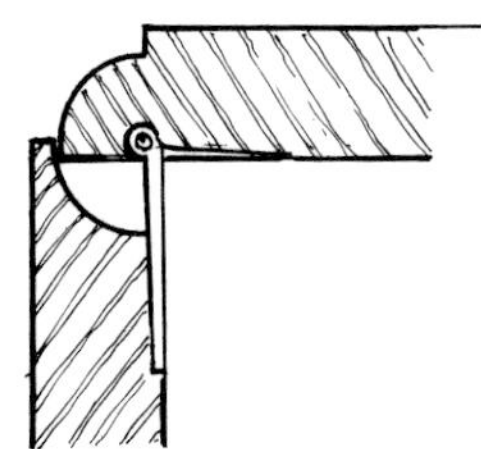

A hinged joint having a rounded edge in the fixed part engaging with a hollow in the edge of the other part. It requires special hinges in which the screw countersinking is on the reverse side from the knuckle so that the centre of the pin is recessed into the wood.

Scratch-stock

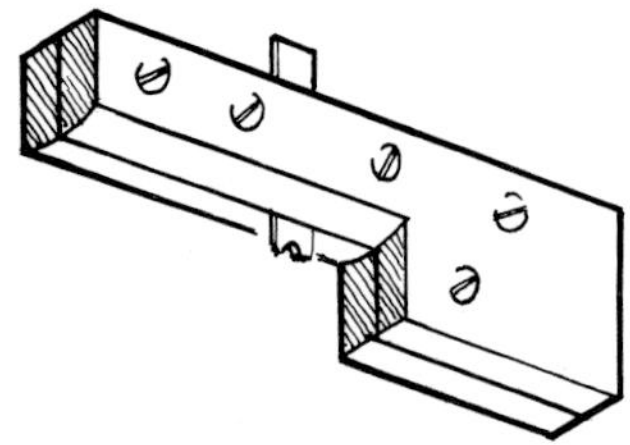

Tool (invariably home-made) used to work mouldings, inlay grooves, etc. The cutter is gripped when the screws are tightened. It can be used in either direction, and has the advantage of not tearing out the grain. Furthermore the groove or moulding can be stopped at any point.

Screw plate

Metal plate with screw at one end. Used chiefly to hold light shelves beneath a table.

Slot dovetail
See under Dovetail.

Steady, lathe

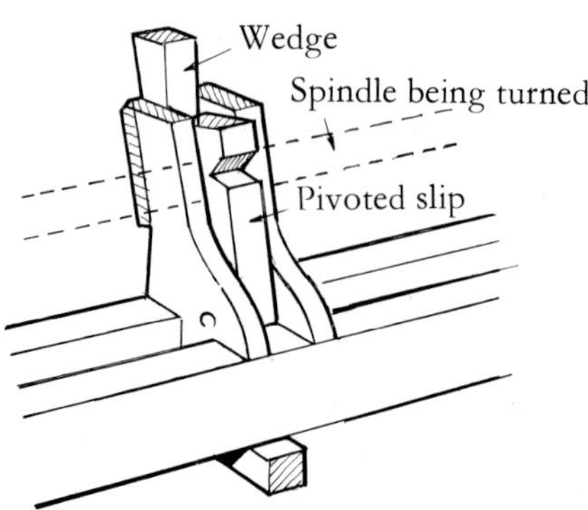

Appliance used by turners when turning long, thin spindles which would be liable to whip. A small portion has to be turned first opposite the steady so that the latter has a cylindrical surface with which to engage. The wedge presses the pivoted slip forwards so that the V notch engages the turning.

Stile
See Door, parts of.

Stuck moulding

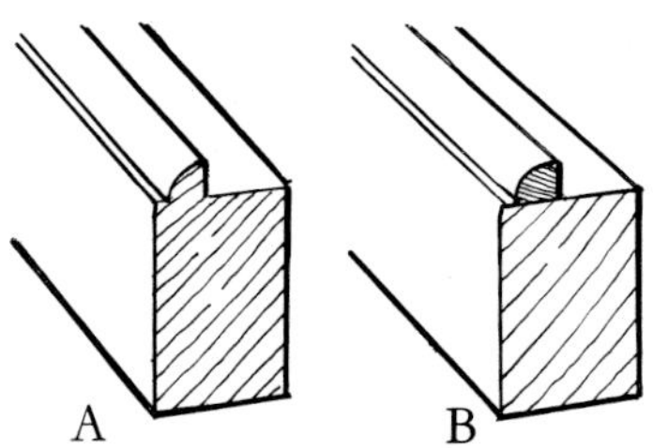

One which is worked in the substance of the item itself (A) as distinct from being worked separately and applied (B).

Through dovetail
See under Dovetail.

Thumb moulding

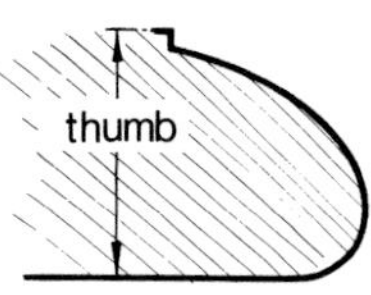

Small rounded moulding.

Veneering hammer

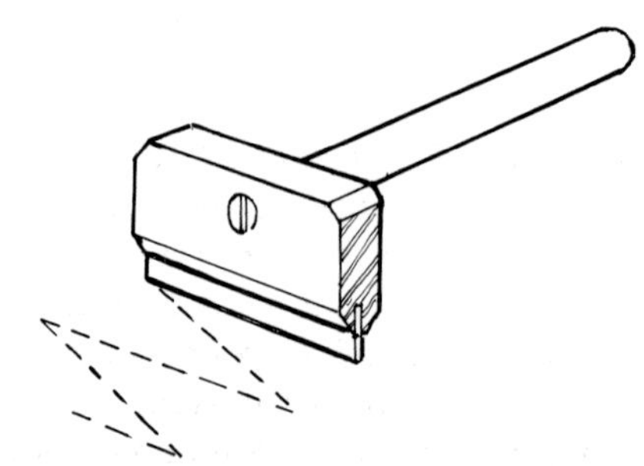

Tool used to press down veneer and squeeze out surplus glue. Main stock is of wood with tongue of brass. See also Hammer veneering.

Water gilt
Type of gilding in which the gold leaf is applied over gesso (q.v.) with a gilder's tip. Gesso is water-based and the gold leaf adheres by virtue of the parchment size or rabbit skin glue in it. It can be brought to a highly burnished finish by the use of the burnishing tool.

Index

Small oak gate-leg table of the middle of the seventeenth century (Victoria and Albert Museum)